F(

Mr Graham Holley had a distinguished career in the Grimsby area finishing as Headmaster of Lisle Marsden Middle School but well remembers his intial start in teaching at Armstrong School

This slice of social history is based largely on personal memories. It is factual and as far as possible accurate and preserves the events and people creating the West Marsh story. Here is an area quite clearly defined by railways and roads and producing an affection and loyalty unusual among urban districts.

Usually when old West Marshites meet, happy memories are recalled often featuring schooldays and the pupils and teachers involved. Sam Smith's book seeks to recapture and preserve the spirit of the West Marsh and to answer questions such as "Who, when and where" with some authority.

Graham Holley

Teacher at Armstrong Street
School 1952 - 1964

Sam Smith

ISBN: 978 1 85749 883 7

Published on behalf of Anthony (Sam) Smith - 6 Radcliffe Road, Healing DN41 7NH - tel 07542 548513
by Pearson Publishing, Chesterton Mill, French's Road Cambridge CB4 3NP

ACKNOWLEDGEMENTS

My sincere thanks go to the following contributors of photographs and memories of the school and staff:

Sheila Copley, Dennis & Barbara Holah, Graham Holley, Valerie Smith, Lesley Lumb, Jean Robbins, Ian Nowell, Peter Wills, Norman Vivins, Len Brown, George Alltoft, John Dixon, Dave Blanchard, Arthur Baxter, Betty Houlton, Charles Merry, Bob Read, Ray Bage, George Moore, Jim Stewart, John Ellerby, John Chapman, Arthur Taylor, Bernard Wilkinson, Barbara Lane, Barbara Coates, Walter Lord, Joan Beasley, Janet Wright, Cynthia Byrne, Sheila Blanchard, Frank Mallinson, Gordon & Norma Gilliatt, Roy Lightfoot, Pete Waters, Roy Walker, Alan Bromley, Ken Brocklesby, Lesley Peatfield, Peter Goulding, Roger Bunn, Jeff Beedham, Alan Jackson, Ron Greenacre, Roy Asher, Colin Last, Ray Hall, Dave Garland, John Abe, Jane Hyldon King, Geoff Lindley, Bob Hogget,

Staff of North East Lincolnshire Council Libraries

John Wilson, Archivist, and staffs of North East Lincolnshire Archives

Peter Chapman, author of Grimsby The story of the World's Greatest Fishing Port

Daniel Smith for compiling subsidence graph data

Grimsby Telegraph for permission to reproduce photos

Daily Mirror for permission to use 1928 photo of Armstrong site

Special thanks go to:

Sandra Mason, Manager, St Hugh's Community Centre, for her encouragement and help in pursuing the project for publication

John Robinson for his professional advice and assistance

Matthew Foster-Smith for his expertise and valuable assistance and time in preparing the book for publication

Jane Foster-Smith for proofreading the final document

Bibliography

Armstrong St School Boys' Logbook

Education Committee Books

Extracts from Grimsby News, Grimsby Evening Telegraph, Bygones,

School Photograph collection and 1955 School Camp documents- property of Mr Ian Nowell

Extracts from records of the Borough of Grimsby are reproduced by permission of the North East Lincolnshire Archives

Contents

Contents

iv

The Armo Academy

On Monday morning, 30th September 1929, the residents of the West Marsh in Grimsby arose to see hundreds of schoolchildren converging from all directions, to assemble together at the brand new school in Armstrong Street prior to starting their education. The school buildings and playground, reverberated with the nervous chatter and laughter of boys and girls and echoed throughout the surrounding streets in the area. The school soon became a catalyst to the community of the West Marsh serving not only the children, but was used as a Polling Booth for local and national elections and also served as an Adult Educational Centre for evening classes. The school continued to educate the children of the West Marsh and serve the community until 1964 before finally closing its doors.

The school, which was built in 1929 for the expanding development of the West Marsh, was intended to be the flagship of modern education with up-to-date modern equipment and building techniques, yet within just 35 years, the building (suffering from subsidence from the outset) was finally demolished. The school, during its reign, served thousands of boys and girls for their education from its opening in September 1929 to its closure in July 1964. See the graph below.

Despite this the memory of Armstrong Street School continues to hold fond memories for scores of Grimsby people years after the rubble has been cleared along with all physical traces of its existence. The school played a very important part in the development of the town and was the place where many well-known Grimsby citizens had received their education. It quickly developed a reputation as a tough school excelling in sports against opposing schools and there was a pride for pupils when they said they attended Armstrong, nicknamed "Armo" or Armstrong Academy.

Years have passed by but the fond affection for the school and its teachers often come into conversation. It was this that gave me

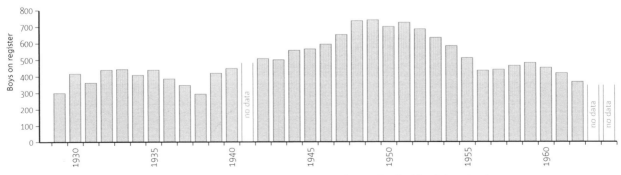

A graph of the Senior Boys school attendance figures for the life of the school

The only surviving photo of the school buildings, taken in 1956.

the desire to write about the school, the great characters on the teaching staff and the influence they had on the destiny of pupils.

The teachers were real characters in their own right and, nowadays you would disbelieve the methods they adopted. In comparison to today's legislation on schooling standards, their actions would be out of line but, having to deal with a class of 45 teenage boys from deprived backgrounds, they had to be in ultimate control. They turned many wayward boys and girls into decent citizens and, years after, are spoken of with gratitude and affection by ex pupils.

Equally it was the aim of the Girls' School to try to turn out girls who can take their places in the world and make a worthy contribution as useful citizens. With this end in view the girls were trained to accept responsibility, to undertake any task with cheerfulness, and to have pleasant and easy manners. The book seeks to show the reader the day to day events and happenings that occurred during this period and the education standards and teaching methods adopted.

The book has been collated using information from records in the archives, newspaper articles and memories from pupils and teachers. It is unfortunate that the book may be biased towards the Boys' School but the majority of information was gained from the Boys' School logbook whereas the Girls' School Logbook has not been deposited in the archives. Despite this the book describes the euphoria of the school when it was built to its ultimate sad end.

This book is dedicated to all pupils and teaching staff who had the opportunity to attend Armstrong Street School and thus became part of the legend of a school long after its demolition.

Sam Smith

1: CONSTRUCTION

On the 24th July 1928 the Grimsby Education Committee sat to discuss their delight on securing the presence of His Royal Highness, the Prince of Wales to lay the foundation stone for the new elementary school being built in Armstrong St School.

The purpose of the visit by HRH the Prince of Wales on 19th July 1928 to Grimsby was to open the new Corporation Bridge before visiting the Docks and Peter Dixon Paper Mills with a final duty of laying the foundation stone to the partly erected Armstrong St School. Ald. Knott, as Chairman of the Education Committee, stated that we were very fortunate as this was the first time that a royal personage had performed such a ceremony at an elementary school and a proposal by Ald. Prior asked whether his Royal Highness had been approached for permission to name the school after him, and suggested "The Prince of Wales Elementary School". There was no opposition to the suggestion. The streets along which his Royal Highness passed had been transformed beyond recognition. Strings of flags strung from house to house in many streets restricted one's view to a few yards. Considerable as were the official decorations,

they were surpassed by the efforts of private persons and businesses. Enlivening the bare appearance of the rising walls of the Armstrong St School were numerous Venetian masts, supporting strings of bunting. The foundation stone ceremony there was performed on a red-decorated balcony under a red canopy. The Prince of Wales was presented with a silver trowel to mark the occasion. Before departing he asked the Mayor to give a day's holiday to all the schoolchildren in the borough.

The following day the headlines in the Grimsby Telegraph read as follows:

- A £50,000 School For Grimsby
- Furnished Flat For Training Future Wives
- Open Air Classes Scheme.

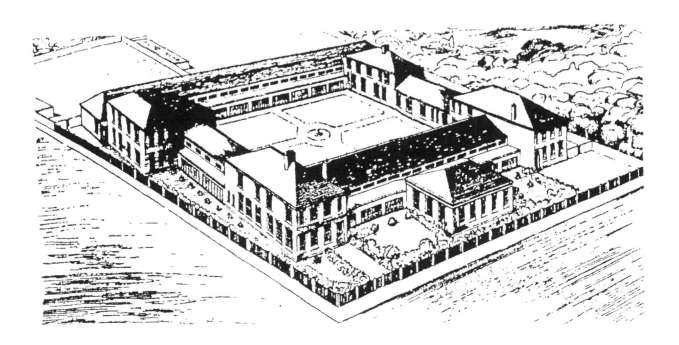

The Foundation Stone

The modern elementary school, with its spacious and well-lighted classrooms, is a palace compared with some of the small, badly lit, insanitary places in which former generations of scholars had to suffer. It is a matter of much discussion as to whether modern educational methods make better scholars, but if environment in the schools has anything to do with it the present day elementary schoolchild certainly has a much better chance than did his forebears. Take for instance, the new school in Armstrong Street and Beeson Street, the foundation stone of which HRH the Prince of Wales laid this afternoon.

Practical training

It will contain a complete small flat, with dining room, kitchen, and two bedrooms, where girl scholars will receive practical training in housewifery. Think what this will mean to their future husbands! The Education Committee, having done so much for the girls, there should be no difficulty in finding them husbands; while the husbands, provided with the complete housewives, will possibly no longer grumble at the call on the rates made by the Education Department. Thus the school will be serving a double purpose.

The provision of this school will relieve much pressure on the South Parade School, and enable the Chapman Street and St. Paul's Schools, which are not the most suitable of buildings, to be closed. The new school will provide accommodation for 1,300 children - 400 boys, 400 girls, and 500 juniors. There will be 26 classrooms, and three assembly halls.

School Clinic

The housewifery centre has already been mentioned, and there will also be a school clinic with a waiting room and doctor's room. The general scheme of building is that now recommended by the Board of Education. The classrooms are erected all round a quadrangle, which enables the building to be turned practically into an open air school. The area of the site is two and a half acres. When the building is finished the chief frontage will face Armstrong Street, where the foundation stone laying ceremony took place today. With the exception of a small one-storey portion at each end of the Armstrong Street elevation, which will contain cloakrooms and teachers rooms, the building will be confined to the ground floor.

Foundation Stone Laying ceromony

No Swimming Bath

In the original plans provision was made for a swimming bath, but the Board of Education, in an economical mood, declined to allow this part of the scheme to be carried out.

Mr. H C Scaping is the architect, and the tender of Messrs. Hewins and Goodhand for the building work amounted to £40,848. Which is equivalent to about £38 per school place?

The cost of the scheme was criticised to a considerable extent when it was first introduced to the members of the Education Committee, but all the members recognised that a school was an immediate necessity in the district.

Extracts taken from the Telegraph 19th / 20th July 1928.

The Opening Ceremony

Fourteen months later, on Thursday, the 19th September 1929, the Earl of Yarborough accompanied by Lady Worsley unveiled the commemorative tablet of the Armstrong Street Council School and officially declared the school open. Having unveiled the bronze mural tablet, which is in the wall of one of the corridors near the main entrance to the girls' department, Lord Yarborough returned to the assembly room and addressed the audience of between 300 to 400 consisting of members of the Grimsby Town Council, and officials, with their ladies, other public ladies and gentlemen and heads of the various schools in the district, while a large crowd assembled outside.

The school was described as the most up-to-date school in the county of Lincolnshire and the Grimsby Education Authority can claim quite legitimately that they have what surely must be the finest and best equipped elementary school in the county. As years go by, and further advance is made in the science of teaching, the merits of the Armstrong Street building may be outdistanced by other erections, but that will not happen for a long time yet, so well have those responsible laid their plans

Alderman Knott in his speech during the school opening ceremony explained that the school would replace two schools, one of which had been in existence for a long time. The Lord St. Mission School opened temporarily seven years ago as an overflow would be closed. The St. Paul's Church of England School, better known perhaps as Chapman St. School was opened as far back as 1877. For over half a century children in the West Marsh and district had been educated at these schools, and expressed appreciation of the wonderful work carried out there under conditions, which, on account of the structure, were not the happiest. The buildings might be a little primitive as many of the older schools were, but the work has been carried on very satisfactorily. This is an age of progress and school buildings in particular were advancing in structure, equipment, and in every way. The curriculum, likewise, has advanced by long strides from the simple instruction, when education was made compulsory about 1874, to a more complex and elaborate system.

Extracts taken from the Grimsby News and The Telegraph 19th /20th September 1929.

A lasting impression

The cost of the new school is £56,000 and is a tribute to local industry. The architect was Mr H C Sparling, and the contractors Messrs. Hewins & Goodhand, who, in building this school, have merely added another to some big works, which include the Wintringham Secondary School, the town's most modern school when built, and most of the important buildings in the town. The work has been done in 18

work has been done in 18 months, although it was expected to occupy two years months, although it was expected to occupy two years. As far as possible local labour has been employed and even the great amount of asphalting necessary has been done by the builders, which also applies to the reinforced concreting and flooring. So often in these big buildings such special work as this goes out of the town. At first foreign doors were specified, but Messrs Hewins & Goodhand persuaded the Education Committee to have local products, which meant a lot of work for local men, who can evidently make very good doors. The whole building suggests that local firms and workmen can, and do, deliver the goals when given the opportunity to do so.

The new school occupies a site of about 11,000 square yards and fronts on Armstrong Street and Beeson Street. Looked at from the outside one gets but a feeble idea of the school. One sees a substantial building set well back from a serviceable boundary paling, which will keep out no light, but the only thing that strikes one is the extraordinary window space. Inside is a very different thing.

The school building itself stands on piles of reinforced concrete sunk to a depth of 35 feet. On these are reinforced concrete foundations, which carry the building. The main fabric is of rustic "Raven head" bricks, and at the entrances, the window sills, and other places it is dressed with terracotta, the whole having a distinctly pleasing appearance. The illustration accompanying this article gives an excellent idea of the disposition of the buildings. These entirely enclose a delightful quadrangle, the fresh green turf being intersected by four paths which leads to a centre circle on which stands a sundial. On three sides corridors open on to this quadrangle, and the first thing the children will see on leaving the classrooms will be this green quadrangle which will also doubtless be used for open air lessons. Behind the buildings are two huge asphalt playgrounds, occupying between them some 7,700 square yards. In each of these playgrounds are sanitary conveniences equipped on the most up-to-date and

one makes the acquaintance of what must surely be the complete elementary school

serviceable lines, caretaker's stores and substantial cycle sheds with sliding doors.

On entering one makes the acquaintance of what must surely be the complete elementary school, for although there is no gymnasium, that green quadrangle and the spacious assembly halls should be all that is necessary for the reasonable physical culture of the children. At once one grasps the idea that the Armstrong Street School is not only a substantial building, but one finished on artistic lines, and with a care that bespeaks pride in the building of it. In the main the corridors have terrazzo — a sort of mosaic stonework —floors, while the classrooms and assembly rooms have wood block floors. Right through the school is a 4ft. 6in. dado of brown glazed brickwork, while above that the plaster, all with a remarkably fine finish on it, is decorated in a delicate blue to the picture rail, above which is a deep white frieze to the white ceiling. Everywhere are ample windows, specially built of vita-glass, which allows the beneficial ultra-violet rays to penetrate so that there shall be the maximum of light and ventilation, with the minimum of draughts — draught is in fact impossible. The whole building is centrally heated, all the pipes and radiators being finished in aluminium paint, and the system being fed from two big boilers in a spacious cellar. The lighting is, of course, electrical.

The school is designed to accommodate 1,350 children and opened with 300 boys, 250 girls and 320 mixed juniors in attendance with the appropriate staff. There are three main departments, with special sections for manual instruction, cookery, laundry, housewifery and a medical clinic. All these departments are so interconnected that any section can be approached from any other without leaving cover, yet any one can be approached from the street without passing through another department. This will facilitate the use of the special departments and the clinic by pupils from other schools.

There are 26 classrooms, all on the ground floor, each practically a replica of the next. The general appearance has been referred to but each has a series of movable blackboards and a spacious cupboard. The furniture is substantial and generally in oak. In the junior department each of the youngsters will have a tiny chair and desk, the folding desks in some of the junior rooms being very neat and handy affairs. Each of the classrooms is about 25ft. by 20ft. in extent and in some of them experiments are being made with special ova and vita glass. The boys' and girls' departments have each an assembly room about 25ft. by 50ft., whilst the junior department has a playroom about 30ft. square, all delightful rooms on the ground floor.

The teachers in each department have very pleasant quarters on the upper floor. The head has a large airy room, whilst the staff has a bigger room still, each of them with one of the latest well grate fireplaces, with an artistic oak surround and over mantel, with mirror complete. There is also Lavatory accommodation on the most up to date lines. The staff quarters are the same in each department as well as roomy stores. The teachers, like the pupils, look like having exceedingly pleasant places in which to rest and work.

The special departments are the most interesting parts of the school and each of them is a self-contained unit. The Manual Instruction Room is on the upper floor of the boys' department. In the main room are ten benches equipped with a vice, etc. The instructor has a little private room, and a spacious wood store at his disposal. The medical clinic is between the girls and juniors departments on the ground floor, and here is a large room for clinical work, with a waiting room adjoining.

The cookery and laundry sections are laid out on the most up-to-date lines. Here is an ordinary Yorkshire range such as met with in most houses, an "Ideal" boiler which will produce the hot water for domestic use and two washing sinks. There looks like being more, for there were fittings obviously internal for both gas and electrical equipment. Nearby is a spacious pantry, with its ventilated meat safe. The whole room is tiled from floor to ceiling, while the floor is of terrazzo. The housewifery section, which is on the upper floor of the girls' block, seems to have been modelled and finished on well-conceived, ideal home lines. In the kitchen, which has a wood block floor, is a Yorkshire range so up-to-date, that the front of the oven door, and the door of the warming cabinet is of special glass, so that one can actually watch the food cooking without opening the oven door. This has a prettily tiled hearth, has its kerb, and will be, like all the other rooms, fully furnished. The scullery, a typical one, with sink and other equipment, has a terrazzo floor and is tiled, while the

What a bathroom!
It would grace a mansion …

roomy larder has two ventilated food safes. There is a bedroom and a bathroom. What a bathroom! It would grace a mansion with its tiled walls, pink terrazzo floor, big bath, hand basin and sanitary appliances. There is plenty of room in this bathroom. Hot and cold water is laid on; in fact this convenience applies right through the school. As one passed each department one noted near the entrance the big airy cloakrooms, each with their hundreds of numbered pegs on a skeleton metal framework which will allow a free passage of air through the clothing. Along one wall is a row of ten or a dozen neat hand basins, whilst in a corner at a convenient height is a drinking fountain worked on novel lines, and making for cleanliness.

Extracts taken from the Grimsby News, Friday, 30th August 1929.

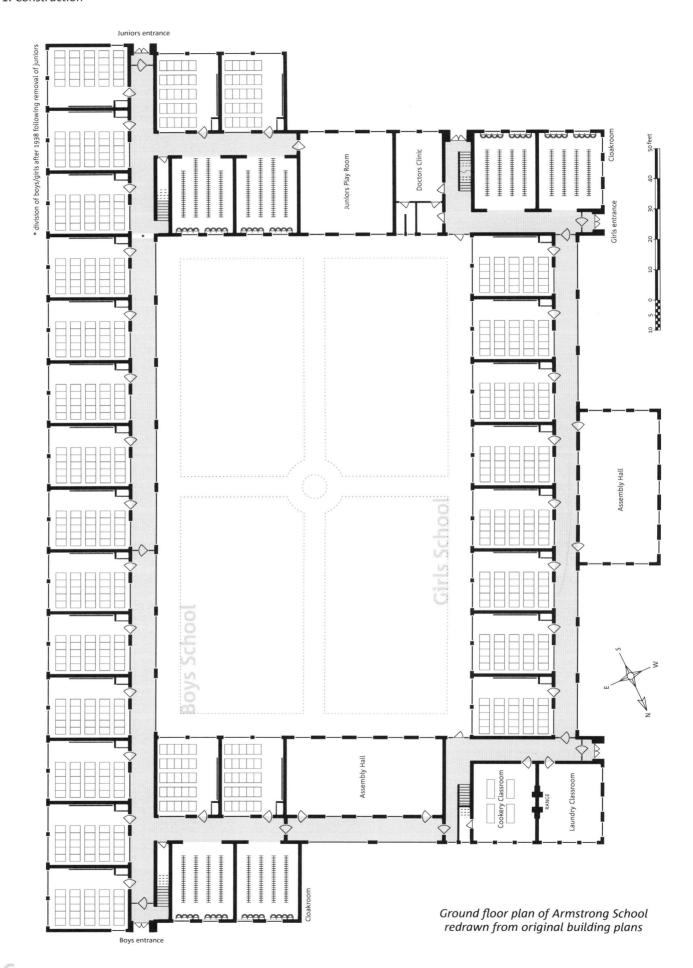

Juniors entrance

* division of boys/girls after 1938 following removal of juniors

Boys entrance

Girls entrance

Juniors Play Room

Doctors Clinic

Cloakroom

Boys School

Girls School

Assembly Hall

Assembly Hall

Cookery Classroom

RANGE

Laundry Classroom

Cloakroom

Cloakroom

50 feet

Ground floor plan of Armstrong School redrawn from original building plans

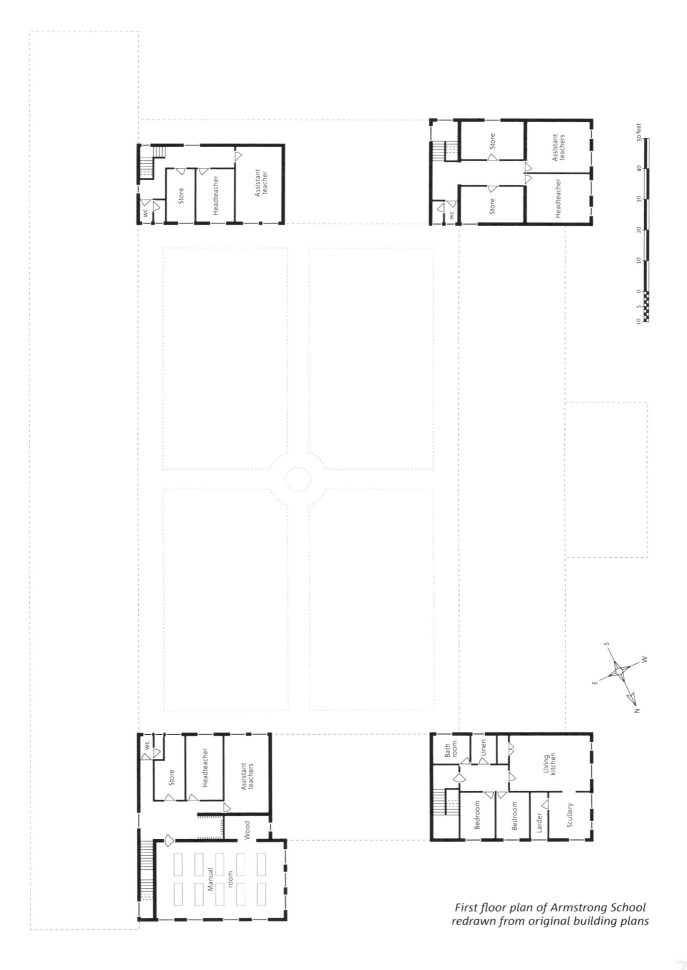

First floor plan of Armstrong School
redrawn from original building plans

COUNTY BOROUGH OF GRIMSBY EDUCATION COMMITTEE.
ARMSTRONG ST. COUNCIL SCHOOL.

No 7.

SOUTH-WEST ELEVATION

NORTH-EAST ELEVATION TO ARMSTRONG STREET

NORTH-WEST ELEVATION TO BEESON STREET.

END ELEVATION OF GIRLS' ASSEMBLY HALL

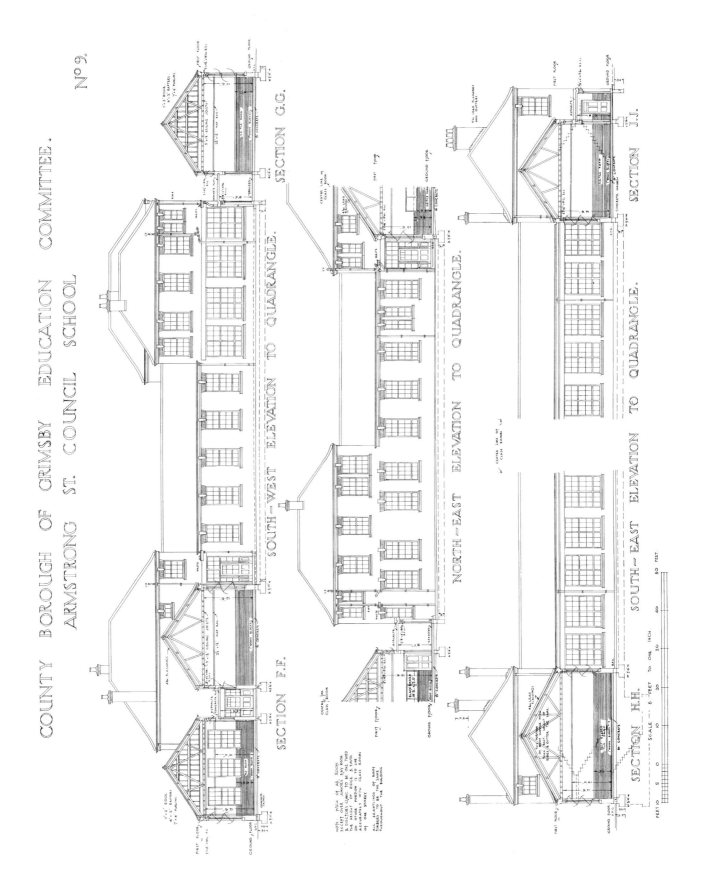

COUNTY BOROUGH OF GRIMSBY EDUCATION COMMITTEE.

ARMSTRONG ST. COUNCIL SCHOOL

N° 9.

SOUTH-WEST ELEVATION TO QUADRANGLE.

SECTION G.G.

SECTION F.F.

NORTH-EAST ELEVATION TO QUADRANGLE.

SOUTH-EAST ELEVATION TO QUADRANGLE.

SECTION J.J.

SECTION H.H.

SCALE — 6 — FEET TO ONE INCH

2: SCHOOL DIARY PRE-WAR

The daily events at the school, including teaching staff absenteism and changes of staff were diligently recorded by the Headmaster in the school's logbook. This chapter contains excerpts from 1929-1939.

1929

30th Sept 1929

This new school building, designated "Armstrong Street" has been opened for occupation today. This department, "Senior Boys" has commenced with exactly 300 boys admitted from St. Paul's Church of England and Lord Street Council Schools, both now closed, and South Parade Senior Boys' School. The ages of the boys are mostly low, and the status of the school is consequently mostly junior. The boys are divided into six classes, six assistant teachers having been appointed to work here, the standard rankings as 2b; 2a; 3b; 3a; 4; 5; 6.

The staff is composed of:

- **Frederick Barnard Potter**, Head Teacher, (St. Paul's)
- **James Henry Kew**, CA, (Harold St. Seniors)
- **Cyril Harper Bristow**, CA, (Harold St. Juniors)
- **Alec Herman Withers**, CA, (Harold St. Junior Boys)
- **Lionel Watson**, (Edward St. Junior Boys)
- **Alfred Beales**, (Harold St. Senior)
- **Thomas Charles Huggins** (St. Paul's)

5th Nov 1929

A further assistant teacher, **Mr Harry Abe**, has been appointed here and commences his duties this morning. The classes have consequently been re-arranged. All but the top class have been disturbed and have been made equal in number, the average number in class being now 43 or 44. Seven classrooms of the eight are now occupied, and the new class created is styled 4b

3rd Dec 1929

Instructions in Life Saving commence this week with 8 boys wishing to attend. 3 cases of Scarlet Fever reported.

A Report on the first general test in Reading, Arithmetic and English

1930

7th Jan 1930

School re opened with all teachers present and 20 children absent. On the instructions of the Education Committee the Handicraft Room is to be used by three sections of boys from Little Coates School. They will attend respectively as follows: Monday 1.30 to 4.00pm, Tuesday 9.00 to 12.00 and Friday 8.45 am till 11.00am.

10th Jan 1930

Harold Kavanagh, who broke his leg in the playground seven weeks ago, is still in hospital, but making satisfactory progress. There are 306 boys on Register. At the request of the Education Committee, a record of the temperatures of each classroom, assembly hall and outside has been made during the past week.

3rd Mar 1930

Wilfred Hugh McCrohan, BA, has been appointed to this school and reported for duty this morning. He will undertake the teaching of English of the two top classes.

31st Mar 1930

Mr T Huggins leaves today, being transferred to Holme Hill Junior Boys' School.

1st April 1930

122 boys have been admitted today, namely 84 from Little Coates and 38 from Macaulay St. These boys are seniors over 11 years of age. There are now 417 boys on register. The eight classes contain from 50 to 55 boys each.

The classification and teachers in charge of the classes are as follows:

CLASS	TEACHER	SUBJECT
1	Mr J H Kew	Geography & History
2	Mr C H Bristow	Mathematics
3	Mr A H Withers	Handwork
4	Mr A Beales	Art
5	Mr McCrohan	English
6	Mr R Watson	
7	Mr H Abe	
8	Mr N W Dingley	Science
	Mr F Potter	Music & Grammar
	Mr Allison	Woodwork

Mr Dingley has commenced work here in place of Mr Huggins. He has been transferred from Little Coates.

After the Easter holidays it is proposed to send 90 boys in 3 sections of 30 each, to swimming at Orwell St. Baths on Monday mornings. There will be 9 sections of 20 each, for woodwork, occupying the room and the Instructor, Mr C H Allison, for the whole of the week except Monday mornings. One section of about 20 is being reserved for gardening, which will take place on Thursday afternoons on the Little Coates' School garden under the superintendence of Mr Kew, the school's gardening instructor.

The School Bank will be conducted by the Headmaster in the Assembly Hall from 9.10am to 9.40am.

19th May 1930

50 boys missing during the afternoon possibly due to the Statute Fair in town.

11th July 1930

The inner entrance door has been removed during the week and replaced by double doors thereby widening the passage for exit. This is a great improvement.

3rd Oct 1930

Attendance remains poor with 50 boys absent today. The numbers on the register is now 383.

12th Oct 1930

An educational visit to the Electricity Works by courtesy of the Chief Engineer was paid by a party of a dozen boys with Mr Bristow.

21st Nov 1930

A group of boys accompanied by Mr Bristow made an educational visit to the Victor Street Ice Factory this afternoon. Previous visits have been made to Thorton Abbey, The Corporation Electricity Works, and the Water Works.

1931

6th Jan 1931

School re-opened with 361 on the register and 23 absent. Two workmen joiners from the North of England Furnishing Co. Ltd. Are on the premises truing window frames.

30th Jan 1931

Owing to bad weather this morning the attendance has been very poor today, early 100 boys are absent.Consequently the average for the week has dropped to 84%.

11th Feb 1931

A doctor of the school medical service attended at the school to examine arms and heads of all the boys for signs of chicken pox, one boy being isolated.

20th Feb 1931

Three cases of Variola Minor have been notified this week by the schools medical officer.

All boys have been inspected by the school dentist. 105 boys absent during the week.

2nd Mar 1931

Mr Leake started his duties here today

1st April 1931

52 boys from Little Coates and 19 from Macaulay St. were admitted giving 408 boys on register.

15th June 1931

14 boys are at Winteringham School all day for the purpose of the Scholarship Exams. School will be closed tomorrow for the annual school Sports Day.

10th July 1931

The terminal exams were concluded today.

22nd July 1931

School closed for summer holidays.

25th August 1931

School re-opened.

4th Sept 1931

Owing principally to the prevalence of rain, the attendance this week is the lowest of the year. Today, a very wet day, 60 boys are absent. Towels were taken to the classrooms and boys were allowed to remove wet stockings and shoes and dry their feet.

30th Sept 1931

Mr Lionel Watson leaves this school and resigns his position today. He has accepted a post at Romford.

23rd Oct 1931

Mr Harry E Potts has been appointed here as replacement of Mr Watson and commenced work this morning.

1932

12th Feb 1932

A conference of the staff was held to decide the policy of organisation for next year, It is decided to continue the policy of specialisation in dealing with the following subjects: Music, Mathematics, Arts & Crafts, Geography & History, and Science. Five groups for five teachers including the Head Teacher. The school will be divided into two groups, each embracing a complete scheme of work, and will be designated classes 1,2,3,4, and 1a,2a,3a,4a.

22nd Feb 1932

A case of Diphtheria, Roy Broddle of 251, Corporation Road, has been notified to me this morning by the Medical Offices of Health.

18th March 1932

The results of the medical examinations are as follows:

126 routine, 8 special, 25 re-inspections, 17 reported for treatment, 1 excluded for Scabies

The classes are organised in two series of 4, designated 4,3,2,1, and 4a, 3a, 2a, 1a.

Class 2a contains 75 boys, and has been divided into two parts, making the ninth class.

Class 1, consisting entirely of new boys and Class 1a, consisting of backward boys, are being treated separately from the general scheme of work.

All classes are concentrating largely on the English side of the scheme.

CLASS	TEACHER	NO OF BOYS
4	Mr Kew	52
3	Mr Bristow	50
2	Mr Beales	50
1	Mr Leake	50
4a	Mr Dingley	50
3a	Mr Abe	50
2a	Mr Potter	31
2a2	Mr Potts	44
1a	Mr Withers	50
	Total	427

2nd May 1932

Mr Roger Warburton commenced work here this morning. Swimming instruction has now begun at the Orwell St. Baths. 90 boys attend in 3 sections of one hour each during Monday mornings.

Awards for Life Saving, practised during the winter months, have been received as follows: Elementary 4, Proficiency 1, Medallion 1.

22nd June 1932

Arrangements were made by the Education Committee to take 340 boys this morning to the Lincolnshire Agricultural Show.

1st July 1932

During an experiment in the Girls' School Practical Room, a scholar, Joyce Bowdler, received an eye injury in consequence of an explosion of a flask.

Sept 1932

The teaching staff were as follows:

CLASS	TEACHER	SUBJECT
4	J H Kew	Geography & History
3	C H Bristow	Maths
2	A Beales	Art & Craft
2.2	A B Leake	Science & Hygiene
4a	R Warburton	Geography & History
3a	H Abe	Maths
2a	H E Potts	Arts & Crafts
2a2	N W Dingley	Science & Hygiene
1	K R Smith	
1a	A Withers	
	C H Allison	Handicraft
	F B Potter	Music

7th Oct 1932

The swimming team has won a Cup this week in open competition, each member of the team receiving a silver medal.

7th Nov 1932

Notification received this morning of two cases of Diphtheria. There are now 440 boys on the register.

11th Nov 1932

This morning, Armistice Day, has been partly used for celebration of Peace. A school service was conducted in the Assembly Hall at which every boy was present, and at 11.00am boys and teachers in the playground observed the silence.

1933

10th Jan 1933

There are 411 boys on register at start of the term.

20th Feb 1933

The records show the course of the Influenza epidemic during the five weeks since Christmas, the percentage being 89%, 71%, 68%, 81%, and 88%.

22nd Feb 1933

A supply of bottled milk, arranged by the Education Committee, has commenced today. Children who want it are bringing one penny each for a bottle, which contains one third of a pint.

12th May 1933

Consumption of milk daily is falling rapidly.

Written application for covered bicycle stand, drinking fountain in playground and gas and water installation in classroom for convenience of teaching science.

6th June 1933

A request for a drinking fountain in the playground was rejected but would have one installed in the cloakroom.

20th June 1933

I have examined the schemes of lessons taught in Geography & History of the top class by the same teacher. I cannot speak too highly of the general plan of the work and the boys response to it. It is the study of man in his enviroment, and the use of official guides and reports make topics alive and fresh.

11th July 1933

A dental demonstration, under the direction of the Dental Board was given, and specimens and models shown to two sections of boys, about 150 in all.

26th July 1933

Yesterday, Thursday, the afternoon

was utilised for the purpose of the school sports which were carried out on the Boulevard Green.

34 boys under the supervision of Mr Leake paid a visit to the Electrical Works.

There are 444 names on the register with 30 boys who are decidedly dull and backward.

The staff is as follows:

CLASS	TEACHER	SUBJECT
	Mr F Potter	Headmaster
4a	J H Kew	Geography & History
3b	H Abe	Maths
3a	C H Bristow	Maths
3b2	N W Dingley	Science
3a2	A B Leake	Science
2b	H B Potts	Art
2a	A Beales	Art
1a	K R Smith	
4b	R Warburton	Geography & History
1b	A H Withers	
	C H Allison	Handicraft Instructor

25th Oct 1933

The Education Committee presented a certificate and medal to Ralph Heaton, who has just left school at 14 years of age, for working 5 years complete attendance and 6 with the exception of half a day.

1934

1st June 1934

Mr Bristow and Mr Beales are taking a small party of boys to Thorton Abbey, leaving at 12.45 in order to catch a train.

Mr Dingley is taking a party of boys to Tealby today until tomorrow. They are utilising no part of school time.

Class 4b accompanied by Mr Dingley paid a visit to the Grimsby Gas Works.

6th June 1934

A boy, Arthur Richmond, was hit on the eye by a stone propelled by a catapult in the hands of another boy, undiscovered.

This occurred in the playground prior to 1.30pm, and has been reported to the Secretary of the Education Committee. The boy was sent home immediately to the parents to seek advice and treatment.

22nd June 1934

While in the playground yesterday afternoon, William Raven, 12 years of age, was bitten by a dog owned by Mr Stephenson of 19 Adam Smith Street and in charge of his son, Albert. The matter has been reported to the Education Committee.

25th July 1934

The annual School Sports was held this afternoon on the Boulevard.

7th Sept 1934

Mr W Harriman joined the staff today from Nunsthorpe.

There are 409 boys registered this term and the teaching staff is:

CLASS	TEACHER	SUBJECT
	Mr F Potter	Headmaster, Music
4a	Mr J H Kew	Geography & History
3b	Mr H Abe	
4a2	Mr C A Bristow	Mathematics
3b2	Mr K R Smith	
3a	Mr A B Leake	Hygiene & Science
2b	Mr A H Withers	
2a	Mr A Beales	Art & Craft
	Mr Allison	Handicraft
1a	Mr H E Potts	
4b	Mr N W Dingley	
1b	Mr W Harriman	mentally retarded
	Mr R Warburton	unattached

4th Oct 1934

School closed in the afternoon on the occasion of the opening of the new Fish Dock.

9th Nov 1934

During the last five days boring operations have been in progress in the ante yard. A noisy engine all day is disturbing, and there is barely room for boys to assemble and to move between the school and the playground. Boring operations ceased on Nov 12th.

23rd Nov 1934

There is an amount of enforced absence owing to broken limbs and other accidents, tonsil removal etc.

30th Nov 1934

School closed for the occasion of the wedding of HRH the Duke of Kent to HRH Princess Marina.

1935

11th Jan 1935

According to instructions received from the Education Committee, the garden at Little Coates is passing from the supervision of the Instructor, Mr Kerss, and its cultivation is being undertaken by this school staff. At the present, Mr N W Dingley Bsc will be the instructor.

4th Mar 1935

Roger Warburton died on Saturday last, March 2nd. He had been absent from duty since the summer holiday of 1934, and has suffered a very long illness.

21st March 1935

The preliminary scholarship exam is being conducted during this morning and tomorrow morning. 71 boys have sat for the exams in English and Arithmetic out of 75 eligible by age, of these 4 boys obtained 75% marks and 12 other boys 60%. Twenty boys including mental deficient obtained below 25%.

17th May 1935

Despite the presence in the district of the annual Statute Fair the attendance has maintained a good level, nearly 94%.

27th May 1935

An accident occurred in the playground at 1.15pm when Clifford Rawlins sustained

a heavy blow on the back of his head and a deep cut in the scalp. This was reported to the Education Committee.

26th June 1935

An accident to Nathan Garland, age 13, by which he hurt his shoulder during a P T lesson, has been reported to the Education Office. The boy is attending hospital and is reported to have sustained a crack in the collar bone and bruises. This boy has previously broken arm bones on five occasions. In future he will not take part in P T exercises.

31st July 1935

Mr A Beales leaves this staff today, after serving here since opening of the school on 29th Sept 1929. He has been transferred at his own request to another school in town.

6th Sept 1935

The Staff and its disposition are as follows:

CLASS	TEACHER	SUBJECT
	F B Potter	Head Teacher, Music
4a	J H Kew	Geography & History
4b	N W Dingley BSc	
4a	C H Bristow	Mathematics
3b	F H Hodgson BA	
3a	A B Leake	Science and Hygiene
2b	K R Smith BSc	
2a	A H Withers	Art and Craft
2b2	H Abe	
1a	J J Sigley	
1b	N Harriman	
	H B Potts	Physical Training
	C H Allison	Woodwork

There are now 440 names on the register.

13th Sept 1935

Two classes 4a and 4a (2), accompanied by two teachers, have visited the local art exhibition this morning.

15th October 1935

During a P T lesson today, while using the long vault, a boy, Harry Clark, 14 years of age, hurt his arm. Seeming to have suffered a possible fracture, he was rendered first aid and taken to the hospital. (Harry Clark sustained a fractured arm which was set and put into plaster of Paris at the hospital)

Another boy, Thomas McArthur, age 13, was also sent to the hospital today with a damaged hand caused by fighting another boy in the playground prior to afternoon assembly.

24th Oct 1935

An orchestral concert given in the Prince of Wales Theatre was attended by 68 boys at a charge of 6d each, accompanied by Mr Sigley.

13th Dec 1935

A total of 45 certificates for distance swimming has been awarded to boys attending swimming classes last summer.

1936

7th Jan 1936

School reopened with 386 boys on register. Two cases of chicken pox, one case of Diphtheria and two boys in hospital

24th Jan 1936

Yesterday, Thursday, two boys, Brian Willis and Tom Fuller were bitten by a dog, both in the hand, while playing in the playground previous to afternoon assembly. Both boys were treated with iodine, and the former sent home and to hospital for further treatment. Both are apparently progressing favourably.

This morning, previous to assembly, Leslie Hargreaves fell while sliding, and broke a collarbone. His arm was put into a sling, and he was sent home, and to the hospital, accompanied by two boys. The accident was reported to the Secretary.

28th Jan 1936

The school was closed this afternoon (1/2 day) on the occasion of the funeral of His late Majesty King George V.

7th Feb 1936

During recreation yesterday, Thursday afternoon, Malcolm Smith of class 2b fell and sustained injury to the front of his neck or throat. The manner of accident or the exact nature of injury has not yet been determined. The boy was sent home, and subsequently taken to hospital by his mother, where he is detained for observation.

30th March 1936

The annual medical examination of all boys of 12 years of age has commenced today.

One boy has been committed by the Juvenile Court to an Approved School, 2 boys have been admitted, one after nearly two years out of school ill, the other readmitted for the second time after spending six months in the Scartho Sanatorium.

27th May 1936

Recently an official of the Board of Education visited and enquired the reason for the comparatively small consumption of milk through the "Milk in Schools" scheme, no notice has been given, and no reasons ascertained, so no definite reply was given, A referendum on the matter taken today gives the following reasons for refusal of milk by 75% of the boys

REASON	RESPONSE %
Poverty	41
Indifference	16
Dislike	22
Superfluity	21
Total	100

29th May 1936

Mr Hodgson leaves this school today for transfer to Scartho Junior mixed school.

28th Sept 1936

The school gardens at Little Coates will be divided into 2 parts, one part being cultivated by boys from South Parade Senior Boys, the other remaining to us. 16 boys will form the garden section.

16th October 1936

A complaint that his son, Thomas, was struck across his face and hurt by Mr K R Smith, his Teacher, was made by Mr Marshall to the Education Committee, whose School Management Committee investigated the charges brought by him, in the presence of Mr Smith and myself - as Head Master - on the evening of Tuesday last, 13th Oct 1936. As a result Mr Smith was censured by the Committee, and forbidden the use of the cane in the future.

1937

5th Jan 1937

The class sizes were reducing as follows:

CLASS	TEACHER	NO OF BOYS
4a	Mr Kew	38
3a	Mr Leake	38
2a	Mr Withers	32
1a	Mr Sigley	25
4b	Mr Bristow	38
3b	Mr Brooks	33
3b2	Mr Dingley	35
2b	Mr Abe	40
2c	Mr Smith	26
1c	Mr Harriman	26
	Total	331

15th Jan 1937

An epidemic of Influenza is increasing the absentee figures; there are now 83 boys absent.

19th March 1937

Mr H Brooks has been transferred to Edward St. Senior Boys' School.

11th May 1937

Tomorrow, Wednesday, will take place the Coronation of His Majesty King George VI and of her Majesty Queen Elizabeth. School closes this afternoon until the morning of Thursday May 20th. The holiday embraces the Coronation and Whitsuntide.

The first floor Woodworking Room

21st May 1937

The School Medical Nurse has commenced today the preliminary examination of boys of 12 years of age.

31st Aug 1937

Mr J J Sigley died during last weekend as a result of a street accident. Four teachers will attend the funeral this afternoon. The class 2b(2) of which Mr Sigley would have been in charge, has been divided between two other classes, 2a and 2b increasing these to 45 each.

Mr Brooks has returned to this school after his transfer for a term at Edward St. School.

CLASS	TEACHER	NO OF BOYS
Headmaster	F B Potter	
4a	J H Kew	41
3b	W Harriman	42
4a2	C H Bristow	39
2b	H Abe	44
3a	A B Leake	42
2c	K R Smith	29
2a	A H Withers	44
1c	H Brooks	22
4b	N W Dingley	43
Physical Training	H E Potts	-
Woodwork	C H Allison	-
	Total	346

Mr Nowell teaching his class

1938

11th Jan 1938

School reopened with 293 boys on the register. Mr John N Armstrong has commenced work in the Woodworking Room and will take the place of Mr Allison who retires in a few days time.

7th March 1938

Mr K R Smith has been transferred temporarily to Welhome Senior Boys' School.

3rd June 1938

Mr K R Smith has now definetely left this school and his name removed from the staff list.

14th June 1938

Mr Dingley with 12 boys are away for one week camping at Hundon Manor, near Caistor.

14th July 1938

The school closed for the annual school Sports Day.

31st Aug 1938

I, **Frederic B Potter** today resign the Headmastership of Armstrong St. Senior Boys School.

I, **Henry Horn,** took over the Headmanship of this school with the following staff:

TEACHER
Mr Kew J H
Mr Dingley N W
Mr Fuller E C
Mr Johnson T W
Mr Ricketts C T
Mr Abe H
Mr Bristow C H
Mr Dixon G R
Mr Lee A L
Mr Hollingsworth W J
Mr Nowell D A
Mr Holmes M M
Mr Leake A
Mr Malborough G F
Mr Withers C H
Mr Armstrong J N

19th Dec 1938

Received notice cancelling appointment of Mr Marlborough to Little Coates and stating that Mr W T Johnson will be transferred to Edward St. School on 10th January 1939.

Armstrong St. Boy's School Teaching Staff 1939
A Leake, A Lee, H Abe, R Dixon, G Malborough, J Armstrong, W Hollingsworth, M Holmes, D Nowell
A Withers, C Ricketts, J Kew, Harry Horn (Headmaster), E Fuller, C Bristow, N Dingley

School Magazine

The pupils at the Boys' School started to produce their own term magazine about 1937 to 1942 and some early copies are still kept as momentoes.

They were printed by means of a Hectograph or "Jelly Bed" method onto ordinary exercise book paper. This method was primitive giving reduced quality with every print as the ink began to fade.

The contents of the magazines were very good with articles submitted by pupils ranging from 11 year old to 13 years in their own handwriting using the scratchy pen nibs supplied at school. Articles were submitted on a range of topics and interests, examples of which include:

How to build an aeroplane from balsa wood, Semaphore signals, Morse code, Poets corner, Crossword puzzles, Picture Puzzles, Jokes, Mystery and Ghost Stories, Editors chat, Xmas present ideas, Xmas stories, First aid,

There were also reports on the progress of the schools football teams and scorers.

The Easter term 1939 reported that the 1st team consisting of Tucker, Oldridge, Brown. Wilson, Butters, Ferguson, Cook, Sargent, Taylor, Alltoft and Joass were in a good position in the league, only losing two matches. They are proud to have two boys in the school team, Butters and Alltoft who have been chosen to play for Grimsby Boys.

Christmas 1940 reported that the 1st team played exceptionally well last year, winning the Roberts Cup, with many of the players in this years squad and as yet still undefeated. The team is:

B Bell, A Hamilton, K Crane, R Courtney, L Hurton, R Hallett, W Ellis, A Douglas, H Haagensen, H Ellis, G Stout.

The 2nd team scorers are listed with Ramshill - 10; Roberts - 8; Hardy - 3; Vivins - 3; Kirk, Dean and Green - 1.

Chess tournaments were also very popular with a league table of players listed. Chess moves were also illustrated in articles along with tips from teacher, C H Bristow.

	PLD	WON	LOST	DRAW
Keyworth	20	17	3	0
Crane	19	15	2	2
Bell	16	13	3	0
Hurton	19	15	3	1
Buffey	15	10	2	3
Grundy	26	18	8	0
Day	16	10	6	0
Norvock	18	11	7	0
Bagley	13	4	6	3
Charlton	14	7	6	1
Simmons	13	4	6	3
King	14	4	10	0

In October 1938 the Magazine reported on a series of lectures introduced by Mr. Abe's class, given by the pupils on a subject of their choosing. The following list illustrates some of those:

- Mr Nurse — Model railways
- Mr Cook — Darts
- Mr Millward — Model aeroplanes
- Mr Bagley — My Meccanno
- Mr Buffey — Stamps
- Mr Fawcett — Jokes
- Mr Day — Chemistry
- Mr Millward — Air Raid Police
- Mr Munro — White mice
- Mr Tyson — General Hobbies
- Mr Turner — Guinea pigs

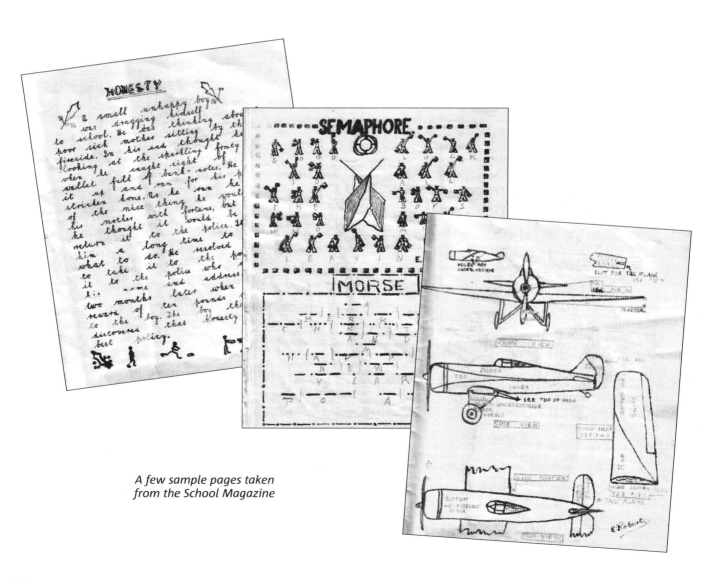

A few sample pages taken from the School Magazine

3: THE IMPACT OF WAR

This chapter describes the Education Committee dilemma in ensuring the safety of the children and their education during the Second World War.

Notes from the Education Committee's books

Grimsby Education Committee received notice on 28th July 1939 of the Government Evacuation Plan No 3. Fortunately, unofficial permission to proceed with the preliminary work in the preparation of a scheme was given at a Conference at the Ministry of Health on 2nd June.

The absence of any information as to the reception areas which would be available for evacuees from Grimsby or the mode of transport which would be used made it impossible to take the scheme as far as the final details.

On Thursday, August 31st, intimation was received from the Regional Office of the Ministry of Health that evacuation under Government Plan No 2 was to take place and that if it was at all possible the Ministry wished to include Grimsby and Cleethorpes in the scheme. A conference was called at 4.30pm that afternoon and invites to representatives from Rural Districts of Grimsby and Spilsby and the Urban Districts of Alford, Horncastle, Mablethorpe and Sutton, Skegness and Woodhall Spa to attend were issued.

The conference was also attended by representatives of the Ministry of Health and the Traffic Commissioners, The Grimsby Transport Manager and a representative of the Lincolnshire Road Car Company were also present. The Chairman and Vice Chairman of the Committee, Alderman Curry and Councillor Abrahams, together with Alderman Beeson, represented the Grimsby Education Committee.

Children wait for evacuation on South Parade Playing Field

As a result of the conference it was decided to carry out evacuation of school children from the evacuation areas of Grimsby by road transport on the following day, Friday, September 1st, and mothers with children under five and cripples on Saturday, September 2nd. Expectant mothers were evacuated on Monday, September 4th, and blind persons on the succeeding days.

Notices to close the schools and evacuation warnings had, in the meantime, been sent to all schools in the Borough, and volunteers were called up for 8.00am on the Friday. A meeting of Head Teachers of evacuable schools was held at 6.30pm on Thursday evening, August 31st, and a further meeting with Head Teachers to be responsible for Assembly Points on the Saturday was held at 9.00pm.

Whilst the numbers of children registered was known, it was thought that these would be increased on the morning of evacuation, but this was not the case, and a considerable proportion of those registered did present themselves at school on the morning of evacuation. Actually only about 60% of the registered numbers were eventually evacuated.

> *Classrooms were deserted, books unread, blackboards scrubbed clean.*

Hundreds of children were going to school blissfully unaware the biggest upheaval of their lives was about to befall them. On 2nd Sept 1939 it was as though the pied piper had been through the town with playgrounds, which the previous day were full of laughter and noise from children, now empty and silent. Classrooms were deserted, books unread, blackboards scrubbed clean. The children were about to be evacuated to the Lincolnshire countryside.

The children left in a fleet of buses, clutching small bags and packets of hastily made sandwiches, a gas mask in a cardboard container around their necks, a label identifying them pinned to their coats. Many parents opted not to send their children; others were only too pleased of the evacuation helping, as it did, their weekly battle to make ends meet. For the children it was an unforgettable experience to be uprooted from crowded streets of Grimsby's West Marsh.

The children who stayed witnessed the erection of Anderson shelters in everyone's backyard. Six foot long by four foot wide, dug down into the garden to a depth of three feet and surrounded by a four inch concrete wall and floor, the corrugated top was about four foot high above ground with just one small door. The shelters often flooded and needed to be baled out. They were to be the bedrooms for a long time, with bunk beds inside. Young married women with small children, worrying about husbands away fighting, also had to struggle to get their children out of bed at any time of the night, winter or summer, always having flasks ready and warm clothing (bearing in mind the children still suffered all the normal illnesses that the young go through). In the shelter all they had for a light was a candle and that was only if they had the door shut, otherwise a voice would boom "Put that bloody light out" as the A R P man did his rounds.

Boys wait patiently to embark for evacuation in front of Grimsby General Hospital and South Parade Methodist Church

The dispatch of the children presented no difficulties. Emergency rations were sent with the parties of children, and in most reception areas the billeting was expeditious. No accidents of any kind have been reported.

The greatest difficulties that have arisen have been firstly, the verminous condition of many of the evacuees and, secondly, the large number of cases of lack of clothing and footwear amongst the poorer section of the evacuated classes. Shortness of time prevented these problems being met in advance and the fact that the evacuation took place only four days after commencement of term meant that the children had not had general cleanliness inspection for over a month and the extent of infestation of the children was astonishing. This problem has been tackled with vigour by

PRIORITY CLASS	EVACUATED	RETURNED
Unaccompanied children	1098	47
Mothers	77	6
Children under school age	175	37
Expectant mothers	34	16
Blind persons	9	2
Cripples	4	-
Total	**1397**	**108**

The extent of the evacuation

the teachers who accompanied the children and the Authorities in the reception area. The lack of clothing is, in some respects, a greater difficulty, and though gifts to supply the deficiency have been received, there are many needs, particularly as regards footwear, that have not been met.

A warm tribute should be paid to the cheerful and ungrudging work of the teachers on the Committee's Staff, to the tolerance of the reception area Authorities and in general, the warm-heartedness of the householders who have taken evacuees.

© Grimsby Telegraph

Front group, left to right: Mr Withers, Mr Fox, Mr H Abe, Mr Nowell (standing), Mrs J Dixon, Mrs E Abe and Mr R Dixon

Arrangements for the education of the children of school age have been made by the reception areas, and such teachers as are not now required have returned to Grimsby.

As instructed by the Ministry of Health, schools in the evacuation area were again opened on Monday and Tuesday, September 11th and 12th and 302 school children whose parents now wish them to be evacuated were registered. Supplementary evacuation will not be carried out until instructions are received from the Ministry. If any such further evacuation takes place, steps will be taken to ensure that each child leaving the town for a reception area is free from bodily uncleanliness and has the necessary equipment of clothing.

The Director reported that in pursuance of the Committee's policy, air raid shelters for schools in the non-evacuable area of the town were being erected, and that the approval of the Board of Education had been received. Formal consent to the borrowing of the sum of £5,604 for a period of twelve years will be issued by the Ministry of Health as soon as possible.

The Director reported that in accordance with the instructions of the Board of Education schools in the evacuable area of the town would remain closed for the present, and submitted the following suggestions with regards to the opening of schools in the non-evacuable area.

Schools to open as soon as the air raid shelters, now in course of construction, are ready for use. For the time being, in accordance with the previous decision of the Committee, only children over 8 years of age to attend. The maximum number of children and teachers to attend at any one session not to exceed the the shelter accommodation available, viz, Nunsthorpe 400, Welhome 250, Carr Lane 200, Edward St. 200, Armstrong St. 200, Macaulay St. 200, Canon Ainslie 50, Scartho 50.

All schools, except Welhome and Macaulay Street, to work a two "shift" system and to be open Monday to Saturday inclusive, 8am To 11.45am, and 12.15pm To 4pm, subject to considerations of daylight in the winter months.

On the 23rd October 1939 Armstrong St School re-opened. The boys from the evacuated areas numbering between 420 – 440 were divided into their original 13 classes and their own teachers visited them in various selected homes, sections vary from 3 to 7 having been arranged to meet at these certain houses. Each class had certain sessions at school so that the specialist lessons could be taken there.

The boys from outside the evacuable area numbering between 60-70 were divided into 2 classes, labelled X and T according to age, X being the elder and consisting of 3rd year boys together with A boys of the 2nd year.

X and T attended school 22.5 hours per week enjoying a full curriculum. Of the staff there are 3 teachers away.

Evacuees waiting for selection to their new homes

War time memories of school

by Mr P Wills

During the early part of the war, enemy bombers used the Dock Tower as a navigation aid before flying over Grimsby onto their targets in the Midlands, and at times, Grimsby docks and shipping became the target for the enemy bombers. They would jettison their bomb load if the intended targets were not found and this caused indiscriminate bombing and strafing of civilian targets in the town. To safeguard the children at school, they were split into two groups, one half attended school in the morning before being sent home at dinner with homework while the other half attended school in the afternoon and again were given work to do at home. Instructions were given to the children in the event of evasive action to be taken if a low flying plane suddenly appeared. In the corridors of Armstrong St School additional fire buckets were available if incendiary bombs were dropped.

The teaching staff consisted of elderly teachers who had served during the First World War and those declared unfit for active service. There was no discipline for lateness as the majority of the town had spent the night in the air raid shelters and pupils would arrive for school lacking sleep. There were occasions, after a heavy night of bombing, when the teacher would tell his pupils to fold their arms and place them on the desk and to lay with their head on them and close their eyes. After a few minutes the majority were asleep and were left by the teacher, allowing them to sleep in their seats.

Clothing was hard to come by during the war, particularly footwear. Clothing coupons were often sold for money and children made do with whatever were available. Holes worn in elbows of jumpers etc was common place and oversize shoes or boots purchased for boys were packed with newspaper to form a fit, steel studs inserted in the soles to reduce wear.

© Grimsby Telegraph

Boys school female teachers
Jess Dixon, Miss Lonerghan, Mrs Radge, Eleanor Nowell

At Armstrong St School the boys had twice weekly lessons on the allotments where vegetables were grown and they also bred Chinchilla Rabbits.

The class sizes were approx 45 pupils and they were given an exercise book for Maths, English and Geography. The Geography teacher had a roller print of the British Isles which he print rolled in each book, and they were taught to put in the rivers, cities etc.

The school building's front entrance, although only built 11 years previously was sinking rapidly and was supported by heavy timbers placed strategically around. The entrance itself was out of bounds to all personnel.

Some of the teachers I recall at Armstrong St School during the war years are:

- **Mr Horn** Headmaster
- **Miss Woodhall** Drama
- **Mr Fuller** Maths
- **Mr Kay** Sport
- **Mr Bristow** Gardening and Chess
- **Mr Merry** Reserve teacher
- **Mr Kew** History
- **Mrs. Nowell** Reserve teacher
- **Mr Leake** Science

Issued by the Ministry of Information *in co-operation with the War Office and the Ministry of Home Security.*

If the
INVADER
comes

WHAT TO DO — AND HOW TO DO IT

THE Germans threaten to invade Great Britain. If they do so they will be driven out by our Navy, our Army and our Air Force. Yet the ordinary men and women of the civilian population will also have their part to play. Hitler's invasions of Poland, Holland and Belgium were greatly helped by the fact that the civilian population was taken by surprise. They did not know what to do when the moment came. *You must not be taken by surprise.* This leaflet tells you what general line you should take. More detailed instructions will be given you when the danger comes nearer. Meanwhile, read these instructions carefully and be prepared to carry them out.

I

When Holland and Belgium were invaded, the civilian population fled from their homes. They crowded on the roads, in cars, in carts, on bicycles and on foot, and so helped the enemy by preventing their own armies from advancing against the invaders. You must not allow that to happen here. Your first rule, therefore, is :—

(1) IF THE GERMANS COME, BY PARACHUTE, AEROPLANE OR SHIP, YOU MUST REMAIN WHERE YOU ARE. THE ORDER IS "STAY PUT".

If the Commander in Chief decides that the place where you live must be evacuated, he will tell you when and how to leave. Until you receive such orders you must remain where you are. If you run away, you will be exposed to far greater danger because you will be machine-gunned from the air as were civilians in Holland and Belgium, and you will also block the roads by which our own armies will advance to turn the Germans out.

II

There is another method which the Germans adopt in their invasion. They make use of the civilian population in order to create confusion and panic. They spread false rumours and issue false instructions. In order to prevent this, you should obey the second rule, which is as follows :—

(2) DO NOT BELIEVE RUMOURS AND DO NOT SPREAD THEM. WHEN YOU RECEIVE AN ORDER, MAKE QUITE SURE THAT IT IS A TRUE ORDER AND NOT A FAKED ORDER. MOST OF YOU KNOW YOUR POLICEMEN AND YOUR A.R.P. WARDENS BY SIGHT, YOU CAN TRUST THEM. IF YOU KEEP YOUR HEADS, YOU CAN ALSO TELL WHETHER A MILITARY OFFICER IS REALLY BRITISH OR ONLY PRETENDING TO BE SO. IF IN DOUBT ASK THE POLICE-MAN OR THE A.R.P. WARDEN. USE YOUR COMMON SENSE.

...EST AUTHORITY AND GIVE HIM THE FACTS.

IV

Remember that if parachutists come down near your home, they will not be feeling at all brave. They will not know where they are, they will have no food, they will not know where their companions are. They will want you to give them food, means of transport and maps. They will want you to tell them where they have landed, where their comrades are, and where our own soldiers are. The fourth rule, there-fore, is as follows :—

(4) DO NOT GIVE ANY GERMAN ANYTHING. DO NOT TELL HIM ANYTHING. HIDE YOUR FOOD AND YOUR BICYCLES. HIDE YOUR MAPS. SEE THAT THE ENEMY GETS NO PETROL. IF YOU HAVE A CAR OR MOTOR BICYCLE, PUT IT OUT OF ACTION WHEN NOT IN USE. IT IS NOT ENOUGH TO REMOVE THE IGNITION KEY; YOU MUST MAKE IT USELESS TO ANYONE EXCEPT YOURSELF.

IF YOU ARE A GARAGE PROPRIETOR, YOU MUST WORK OUT A PLAN TO PROTECT YOUR STOCK OF PETROL AND YOUR CUSTOMERS' CARS. REMEMBER THAT TRANSPORT AND PETROL WILL BE THE INVADER'S MAIN DIFFICULTIES. MAKE SURE THAT NO INVADER WILL BE ABLE TO GET HOLD OF YOUR CARS, PETROL, MAPS OR BICYCLES.

V

You may be asked by Army and Air Force officers to help in many ways. For instance, the time may come when you will receive orders to block roads or streets in order to prevent the enemy from advancing. Never block a road unless you are told which one you must block. Then you can help by felling trees, wiring them together or blocking the roads with cars. Here, therefore, is the fifth rule :—

(5) BE READY TO HELP THE MILITARY IN ANY WAY. BUT DO NOT BLOCK ROADS UNTIL ORDERED TO DO SO BY THE MILITARY OR L.D.V. AUTHORITIES.

VI

If you are in charge of a factory, store or other works, organise its defence at once. If you are a worker, make sure that you understand the system of defence that has been organised and know what part you have to play in it. Remember always that parachutists and fifth column men are powerless against any organised resistance. They can only succeed if they can create disorganisation. Make certain that no suspicious strangers enter your premises.

You must know in advance who is to take command, who is to be second in command, and how orders are to be transmitted. This chain of command must be built up and you will probably find that ex-officers or N.C.O.'s, who have been in emergencies before, are the best people to undertake such command. The sixth rule is therefore as follows :—

(6) IN FACTORIES AND SHOPS, ALL MANAGERS AND WORKMEN SHOULD ORGANISE SOME SYSTEM NOW BY WHICH A SUDDEN ATTACK CAN BE RESISTED.

VII

The six rules which you have now read give you a general idea of what to do in the event of invasion. More detailed instructions may, when the time comes, be given you by the Military and Police Authorities and by the Local Defence Volunteers ; they will NOT be given over the wireless as that might convey information to the enemy. These instruc-tions must be obeyed at once.

Remember always that the best defence of Great Britain is the courage of her men and women. Here is your seventh rule :—

(7) THINK BEFORE YOU ACT. BUT THINK ALWAYS OF YOUR COUNTRY BEFORE YOU THINK OF YOURSELF.

(52194) Wt. /   14,300,000 6/40 Bw.

4: SCHOOL DIARY 1939-1945

Extracts taken from the school's logbook covering the period of the Second World War

20th Feb 1939

A boy, Albert Needham whilst at P T fell over a bench and fractured his arm. The boy was sent to hospital. Mr R Dixon was in charge of the class at the time of the accident.

1st April 1939

Held an Arts and Crafts Exhibition in the school Hall. The work comprised art, manual- handwork and was seen by the whole school, boys and girls, and 78 parents attended. Also we were pleased to entertain the wives of members of the staff.

21st June 1939

Attended meeting at Office at which the Director informed me the plans for evacuation. Held a Staff meeting to inform staff with evacuation plans.

23rd June 1939

35 boys with three teachers, Messrs Lee, Nowell and Dixon bussed to Saltfleet to spend the week in camp.

6th July 1939

Lecture given to leavers by an official of the Ministry of Labour on suitable careers for boys. The lecture was from 10.45 to 11.45 and classes were suspended for this period.

13th July 1939

School closed all day for Sports Day.

14th July 1939

The school won the boys' Championship Cup with a total of 24 points.

The War Years

31st Aug 1939

Received warning notice for evacuation. Only the boys agreeing to evacuation to attend school on Friday. School closed.

23rd Oct 1939

School re-opened. The boys from the evacuated areas numbering between 420-440 were divided into their original 13 classes and their own teachers visited in the homes, sections varying from 3 to 7, having been arranged to meet at certain houses.

Each class had certain sessions at school so that the specialist lessons could be taken there. The boys from outside the evacuable area numbering between 60-70 were divided into 2 classes, labelled X & T according to age, X being the elder and consisting of 3rd year boys together with A boys of the second year.

X & T classes attending school 22.5 hours per week enjoying a full curriculum. Of the staff there are three teachers away: Mr E C Fuller, Mr R Dixon at Skegness, and Mr W Hollingsworth at Hogsthorpe.

24th Oct 1939

Mr J S Pritchard reported for duty. He is on probation and will take charge of 1b and specialise in English with class X. Mr R Walker, Head of the Boys Unemployment Centre reported for duty. He has taken charge of 2b. The attendance for the week with the exception of Saturday has been consistently good; Saturday's drop is due to the fact parents employ their children

© Peter Chapman

Evacuees prepare to leave, carrying a gas mask around their neck, and a small suitcase clutched in their hands

to run errands etc. The attendance on Saturday afternoon was incredibly bad, only 30% of the available children attended.

20th Nov 1939

New timetable being either 8.30am to 11.45am or 12.30pm to 3.45pm. There are now 7 classes in school at one time.

2nd Dec 1939

it was reported that attendances were shocking with Y class in the afternoon having only 7 boys out of 27 in attendance. The morning X class had 13 present out of 22 boys.

16th Dec 1939

Again the Saturday afternoon attendance, which is farcical, 4 present in T Class when the average for the week was 22. In the morning this attendance was 11 instead of an average for the rest of the week, which was 19.

1940

January 1940

Baths were started at the college. 120 boys put their names down. These were divided into 2 sections meeting at their various stated times at South Parade, Boulevard and being marched down.

12th Feb 1940

Mr Fuller resumed duties at school after being away on evacuation duty at Skegness since 1st Sept 1939.

4th March 1940

Started new Timetable 8.15am to 12.15pm; 2.45pm to 4.45pm.

Brought more classes into the school thus reducing the visits paid to the houses.

A section of the boys started gardening at Little Coates School under the direction of Messrs Dingley and Nowell whilst another section under Mr Ricketts started in Lansdowne Ave. I might add that Mr Ricketts obtained the land himself.

© Peter Chapman

Mr Abe and Mr Nowell supervise the evacuation

2nd April 1940

School reopened for full time instruction with 448 boys on register and 430 in attendance. School was organised in 11 classes:

- **Year 1** – A1, A2, B1, B2, C
- **Year 2** – A, B1, B2, C
- **Year 3** – A, B

Mr R Walker returned to his duties at the Junior Instruction Centre.

The days of swimming instruction has changed from Mondays to Tuesday mornings and Friday afternoon

18th April 1940

Owing to a false air raid alarm a number of boys were away from school.

14th May 1940

Whit holidays cancelled owing to serious war news.

18th May 1940

Attended school for evacuation purposes on Saturday morning. 295 boys present out of 444. No registers marked. The following teachers attended:

- Mr H Stillen – Nunsthorpe
- Mr E Smith – Welholme
- Mr Pindepress – Nunsthorpe
- Mr R Hemmingfield – Welholme
- Mr Hutton – Nunsthorpe
- Mr A Walsham – Nunsthorpe

4th June 1940

Harry Thortersen fractured his arm in a P T lesson whilst vaulting over the box. The accident occurred at 11.40am and the boy was sent to hospital.

6th June 1940

In consequence of raid in the early morning there was a very low attendance, 150 boys being away.

7th June 1940

Another raid resulted in 220 boys away. Attendance for week 79%.

17th June 1940

192 boys present, 250 boys absent owing to air raid in the night.

25-26th June 1940

Suspended specialist lessons on both mornings in consequence of raids.

8th July 1940

On Sunday 29 boys were evacuated to Gainsborough with Mr Ricketts.

Mr R Fox received his call up papers thus leaving his post.

28th July 1940

Half the school is in attendance of each session for a month. This week the 2nd year boys were present and in the afternoon the 1st year. This will be changed the following week. Half of the staff is away on a fortnight's holiday, those presently away are -

Messrs Lee, Holmes, Abe, Withers, Marlborough, Leake, and Dingley.

Those at school are – Messrs Fuller, Bristow, Kew, Ricketts, Nowell and Armstrong.

19th Aug 1940

Mr Hollingsworth reported back from Hogsthorpe.

26th Aug 1940

Mr Dearden joined the staff from Holme Hill School.

12th Sept 1940

Air raid warning at 11.45am lasting until 1.20pm. No school in the afternoon.

School won the Hewitt Shield and Maddock Cup at Inter School Swimming.

18th Oct 1940

Mr Marlborough finished today being under orders for munitions work at Leeds.

13th Nov. 1940

Mr J N Armstrong finished today being under orders for munitions work at Leicester.

1941

17th Jan 1941

20 boys aged 13-14 left today having won scholarship at the Technical Commercial Examination at the Municipal College. This result was an extraordinary good one, for this department obtained 20 scholarships out of 57.

20th Jan 1941

Attended meeting at Education Offices for the purpose of discussion upon the duties of teachers as fire guards in their schools.

27th Jan 1941

Air raid alarm lasting 10 minutes from 2.20pm to 2.30pm.

4th Feb 1941

In afternoon, on orders, examined gas masks.

5th Feb 1941

After last night's long raid, in consequence of the poor attendance, the timetable was suspended for the morning.

26th Feb 1941

Cinema Lecture by the Ministry of Information seen this morning by the whole school.

27th Feb 1941

No session in afternoon owing to air raid warning 1.10pm to 2.15pm.

3rd March 1941

The school session in the afternoon is now from 1.30pm to 4.00pm.

The lessons are from 1.30-2.20; 2.20-3.05; 3.05-3.15 and 3.15-4.00

7th March 1941

Air raid warning at 2.45 so let boys home in twos and threes with instructions to run home after 4.00 o'clock. The risk seemed to be very slight, as no raiders seemed to be overhead any part of the period.

12th March 1941

Air raid warning at 11.30.am lasted 10 minutes and turned out to be a false alarm.

25th March 1941

Air raid warning at 3.50 until 3.55pm.

1st April 1941

Air raid warning at 3.30pm.

2nd April 1941

Raid warning as school was dismissed at 11.45am

7th April 1941

Mr Lee absent attending Home Guard course.

9th April 1941

Mr Kew returned to school today.

16th May 1941

Air raid at 3.00pm all clear at 3.15pm.

26th May 1941

Mr A L Lee absent by orders of the School Medical Officer in consequence of his daughter contracting Scarlet Fever.

30th May 1941

Mr Norman Dingley, after 11 years service, left the services and duly transferred to a school in Buxton.

3rd June 1941

Mrs Wright, supply teacher, reported for duty this morning.

17th June 1941

Mrs Nowell, supply teacher reported for duty.

20th June 1941

Mr R Dixon, member of this staff, who has been at Skegness since the beginning of the war, leaves the service of the Education Committee today having joined the RAF as a P T Instructor.

1st Sept 1941

Mrs Dixon and Mrs Nowell were placed on the staff and Mr M Holmes in the holiday joined the RAF as a Pilot Officer.

2nd Oct 1941

Air raid warning from 2.50pm to 3.20pm.

10th Nov 1941

No baths today owing to a visit by the Food Authority to issue Ration Cards. Air raid warning 1.26pm to 2.45pm.

1942

2nd Feb 1942

Alert sounded at 1.45pm; all clear at 2.20pm. All boys during this period were in shelters under the supervision of staff.

5th Feb 1942

No school session this morning. Alert sounded 9.05, all clear 9.45am. Staff remained on duty for the complete session. Alert sounded 3.00pm. Shelter cover as usual.

6th Feb 1942

Alert sounded 1.18pm, all clear at 3.05pm. All boys who were about the school buildings were in the shelters for the period.

17th Feb 1942

Air raid warning at 2.40pm for half an hour.

18th Feb 1942

Air raid warning from 9.35 am to 10.05am and 1.26pm to 2.10pm.

Mr H Abe called to the colours (RA) today

26th Feb 1942

Mr W D Hollingsworth called up for service in the Army (RA).

Air raid warning 2.00pm to 2.15pm.

3rd March 1942

Air raid warning 9.06 am to 9.20am.

9th March 1942

Air raid warning 10.45am to 11.40am.

20th March 1942

Mr N Dearden reported for duty in the Reconnaissance Corp.

27th April 1942

Air raid warning 3.10pm to 3. 30pm.

11th May 1942

Air raid warning 3.25pm to 4.00pm.

12th May 1942

Air raid warning 3.40pm to 3.55 pm.

18th May 1942

Mr H Goulding reported for duty.

Air raid warning from 3.00 for 20 minutes

21st May 1942

Held the 2nd Rabbit Show, opened by Mr Richardson of Education Dept.

26th May 1942

Mrs May C Wright reported for duty.

5th June 1942

All gas masks have now been inspected and defective ones replaced or mended.

1st July 1942

Mrs M C Wright left services of Education Committee.

Mrs Woodhall reported for duty.

13th July 1942

Nine boys were successful in the Technical Exams: Daniel Banks, Norman Wright, George Brocklesby, Geoffrey Hames, Roy Thompson, Robert Harwood, Gerald Thacker, Leonard Harvey, Derek Stubbs.

25th July 1942

Owing to the" All clear" not sounding until 8.55am, The attendance was scarce at 9.10, but improved later on. Moreover the weather was so bad that lessons were out of the question.

3rd Aug 1942

Opened for voluntary attendance. Seven children and seven teachers in attendance.

5th Aug 1942

Closed school for summer vacation.

31st Aug 1942

Reopened school with 507 boys present with two new teachers, Mr S W Kay, Mr C W Merry This made up 14 class teachers for 13 classes.

5th Sept 1942

Air Raid warning 1.50 till 2.15.pm.

12th Sept 1942

The winter sessions of the Baths was started today. The First were from 9.15am to 3.pm. Six sessions of about thirty boys were sent accompanied by a teacher.

6th Nov. 1942

Held highly successful Rabbit Show. Now 300 Rabbits from boys were shown.

3rd Dec 1942

Both Football teams A & B were in the final of Roberts Cup. A team winning 4 - 0. The final quite unique in having two teams from same school. A collection for the Red Cross resulted in the Two Captains taking £4 -10 shillings to Headquarters.

1943

7th Jan 1943

Mr G Leake transferred to Carr Lane Mixed Seniors.

20th Jan 1943

145 boys and 5 teachers attended Philharmonic Concert at Central Hall in afternoon from 2.20pm.

Mr Nowell absent, suffering from jaundice.

10th May 1943

Owing to Macaulay St. Mixed School overcrowding, 65 scholarship year boys have been transferred a term earlier than normal and have been divided into two classes dependent on their IQ 1st June 1943.

Mr C Ricketts transferred to Edward St Senior Boys'.

Mrs. Rudge commenced duties today.

Night of 13th June – 14th June 1943

Blitz on Grimsby. Two dozen Incendiary bombs fell on the school. Very little material damage done as Firewatchers was able to quench their fires.

16- 18th June 1943

Whit holidays extended due to to prevalence of dangerous bombs in the neighbourhood of schools.

21st June 1943

School reopened with 84% attendance. No Victoria St. boys as they had been evacuated owing to bombs.

21 June 1943

8 boys passed the Technical Examination.

13th July 1943

Owing to another blitz on Grimsby the attendance was poor.

14th July 1943

Registers marked but no specialist work done owing to very poor attendance: 280 out of 500.

15th July 1943

Admitted 60 boys from South Parade School, which had been blitzed. These 60 boys were those who were due to come up in August.

30th Aug 1943

Miss Allen on probation joined the staff.

Owing to bomb damage at South Parade, one of that school's classes has occupied a room at this school, thus the Manual Room has been converted into a classroom. The South Parade class is still under its own Head and counts still as a South Parade Class.

1st Dec 1943

Miss G C Allen transferred to Senior Girls' Department.

10th - 20th Dec 1943

Mr Withers absent by permission to attend Sea Cadets course at Portsmouth.

1944

10th Jan 1944

Re-opened school, 13 classes plus
one class from South Parade.

12th Jan 1944

The Director addressed a massed meeting
of teachers upon the new Education Bill.

8th March 1944

Ten boys were successful in the
Technical Exams and were:

Charles Everitt, Harold Forrester, Stuart
Sharpe, Peter Shackleton, Cyril Rees, John
Bradshaw, Robert Drury, Peter Sanderson,
Terence Willey and Neville Giles.

15th Mar 1944

Closed school at 11.45 and 3.30pm as no
coke was available for heating the school.

30th March 1944

At 3.30 220 boys were marched to Clee
Fields to see the Final of the Cup.

5th April 1944

Atkinson Cup presented to the school
by School Sports Association.

12th April 1944

The following eight boys have passed
the scholarship for technical:

Geoffrey Bancroft, Roy Belding, Arthur
Cook, Edward Dennis, W Quickfall, Harry
Shepherd, Alan Stones, Phillip Tyson.

22nd June 1944

School closed for school Sports Day.

June 1944

At Inter school Sports; the school won both
the Senior and Junior Boys. The Senior
competition was outstanding winning
four out of five events, Armstrong A
winning four firsts. Altogether this school
obtained scoring 22 points out of 24.

14th July 1944

Held School Rabbit Show on Saturday
on the Quadrangle. £175 raised.

26th July 1944

Mr C Merry placed on permanent staff.

Mr S W Kay left services of Education
Committee to take a Headship at Frode.

28th Aug 1944

Opened school with 557 boys on book. Miss
Lonerghan on the staff from Strand St.

5th Sept 1944

Mr R Leafe on the staff from
Thrunscoe School, Cleethorpes.

26th Sept 1944

32 boys were sent for potato
picking from 3b classes.

1945

5th Feb 1945

School closed on account of no heating.

7th March 1945

The following boys were successful in
the Building Exams: Dennis Kendell,
Kenneth W Scott, Jack Belderson, Anthony
Bell, Terence C Pearson, John C Field.

David Clegg of 2a obtained a
special place to the Colleges.

25th April 1945

Mrs Eleanor Nowell absent
owing to daughter's illness.

7th May 1945

9 boys passed the Technical Examination,
namely, Harry Briggs, Derek Cole, Robert
Charles, W Davison, Fred Ottoline,
Ronald Peers, Ronald Nurse, David
Tyson and Fred White. This brings
the total scholarships to 100.

8-9th May 1945

V E Day. School closed for two days. End of European War.

10th May 1945

School reopened with 200 boys absent. Timetable suspended as attendance still poor.

18th May 1945

Held Victory Party in afternoon.

21st June 1945

The school again won the Senior Boys' Championship Cup and recorded a record jump of 15ft 7 inches.

5th July 1945

School closed for General Election.

30 boys with teachers Mr Lee and Mr Nowell went to Holton Le Clay for a weekend camp.

10th Sept 1945

Re-opened school with 566 boys on the register divided into 13 classes.

Mr R Dixon has rejoined the staff.

25th Sept 1945

38 boys from 3b (2) and 3b (3) were given leave to help farmers

8th Nov 1945

38 boys returned to school after given leave to help farmers in potato picking.

15th Nov 1945

Mr Hollingsworth reported for duty after service in the forces.

19th Nov 1945

Mr H Abe reported back for duty. Mrs Rudge sent to Nunesthorpe Infants.

26th Nov 1945

Mrs Dixon transferred to Armstrong Girls' School.

Girls' School Victory Party in the quadrange - 18 May 1945

5: SCHOOL DIARY POST-WAR

Extracts taken from the school's logbook covering the period from the end of the Second World War until the school's closure in 1964

12th March 1946

The following boys passed the Building Examination: Edwin Boyington, Keith Robson, Brian Wardle, Derek Alcott, Kenneth Simes, Norman Harrison and Terence Anderson.

26th Feb 1946

Class 3b paid a visit to W Ogles' timber factory accompanied by Mr Marlborough and Mr Fuller.

Mrs Nowell was transferred to Welholme Junior Girls' to start 4th March.

22nd March 1946

The school was renamed as Armstrong Street Secondary Modern School.

Two choirs from 3rd year and second year attended and competed in a Music Festival at the Central Hall. They were accompanied by Mr Leake, Miss Lonerghan and Mr Horn.

17th April 1946

Miss Lonerghan transferred to Nunsthorpe.

20th May 1946

Mr M Holmes rejoined the staff after war service.

17th June 1946

A party of 24 boys out of 3a and 4a accompanied by Messrs Lee and Nowell started on an educational visit to Stratford upon Avon for one week. They will attend the Theatre to see Henry Vth and Macbeth. During the day they will visit places of historical interest connected with Shakespeare and a visit to Warwick is intended.

Mr Norman Dearden reported back for duty after his services in the forces.

20th June 1946

A choir of 41 boys with Mr Leafe competed at Cleethorpes Festival in the morning and 69 boys in the afternoon.

1st July 1946

Mr Fox reported back for duty after 6 years war service.

2nd July 1946

10 boys passed the Technical Examination: Byron Austwick, John Allenby, Thomas Bell, Sidney Lamb, Leonard Dowle, Keith Lill, Peter Ottley, Robert Scott, Royce Stafford and Alan Trought.

8th July 1946

Mr G H Chapman Bsc reported for duty.

9th Sept 1946

School re-opened with 594 boys on register. Mr Armstrong reported for duty after returning from Government War work.

A party of 50 boys with teachers, Messr. Leake and Fuller attended a Musical Festival at Nottingham. The boys were away the whole day and according to instructions from the office were marked as absentees.

5th Nov 1946

Mr J H Kew left school today after being a member of the staff since the school opened 17 years ago.

6-9th Dec 1946

Mr G R Dixon away by permission to report to Oxford for hospital treatment

1947

10th Jan 1947

Mr W R Leake and several boys were away for two days at Manchester Broadcasting as part of a Grimsby Choir in the Children's Hour.

25th Jan 1947

Mr Malborough absent due to Influenza and the whole school suffering with the epidemic with 140 boys absent.

During January and February the school was closed several times due to no heating.

17th March 1947

Mr Chapman transferred to Nunsthorpe.

21st April 1947

The following boys have passed the Building Exam: Charles Briscoe, Brian Dixon and Peter Rodgers.

The successful boys passed for Technical were Brian Addison, Harold Bett, George Booth, Leonard Davies, Gordon Tate and William Taylor.

30th June 1947

A party of 30 boys with two teachers visited Mr E Bacons Trawling Works on the fish docks.

24 boys with two teachers left in a bus for Stratford upon Avon.

Gordon Barwood won a scholarship in the Commercial Examination.

5th Sept 1947

School opened with 652 boys with 14 class teachers averaging 50 in a class.

6th Oct 1947

Mr P C Chessman joined the staff.

Mr Chessman later abandoned his teaching career, and become famous as an actor under the name Patrick Wymark. He featured in many films and TV series, including *The Plane Makers* and *Where Eagles Dare*.

20th Nov 1947

Marriage of Princess Elizabeth, day's holiday

1st Dec 1947

Mr Donald Arthur Hotchkin commenced duties this morning.

10th Dec 1947

The school obtained first out of 54 events in the School Swimming Gala. It is somewhat unique for one school to possess the Football, Cricket, Sports and Swimming Trophies

1948

7th Jan 1948

Reopened school after holidays with Mr P Chessman leaving the staff and Mr C Herbert and Mr D Bateson joining the staff.

18th March 1948

The following boys passed the Building Examinations: Gordon Casseral, Colin Dobbs, Barry Green, David Havercroft, Martin Nurse, Richard Ranyard, Hewsen Rayner, Ronald Thompson.

Edwin Barrett won the Special Place Exam and leaves for Carr Lane G School.

5th April 1948

The following boys were successful in passing the Technical Examinations: T Bunn, Raymond C Genney, Peter C Barsted, Kenneth J Glover, Rodger Cave, James T Tuplin.

Holiday in the afternoon for His Majesty's Silver Wedding.

10th June 1948

Party of 24 boys and 2 teachers bussed to Stratford upon Avon for a camping educational visit.

10th June 1948

Drama class won Cleethorpes Festival with play "Midsummer nights Dream".

The Athletic Cup was again won by the

school obtaining 783 points, a lead of 25 points over 2nd placed school.

1st July 1948

20 boys with teachers Mr Withers and Mr Marlborough left for a school trip to Paris.

6th Sept 1948

I, John Holmes, took over the appointment of Headmaster of Armstrong Secondary Modern Boys' School from Mr H Horn, with 18 assistant masters: Mr Lee, Nowell, Withers, Goulding, Hayes, Hollingsworth, Holmes M, Dearden, Marlborough, Fox, Armstrong, Hotchkin, Herbert, Bateson, Dixon, Abe, Leake, and 1 new appointment C H Coleman.

There were 736 boys on the register divided into 16 classes. The school except the Assembly Hall has been internally decorated in the holidays.

15th Oct 1948

A football match between the school's A team and the staff was played at 4.15pm at Littlefield Lane in aid of the "Harry Horn" presentation fund. Great interest was shown. There was a good crowd and the staff won 6-1.

5th Dec 1948

The school A team won the Roberts Cup by defeating Elliston by 2 goals to nil on LNER Ground, Carr Lane.

6th Dec 1948

Mr C A Forde joined the staff.

16th Dec 1948

An assembly of the upper school was held at 3.15pm and attended by Mr Horn, late Headmaster with a presentation for his service to the school. Head Prefect, R Riggall presented Mr Horn with 4 trophies which he gave to the school for internal sports competitions.

1949

10th Jan 1949

Mr D Bateson having left during the holiday, his form was taken over by Mr Forde.

The school total was 682. The classes were reorganised to give lower numbers and changes in the timetables to allocate Games and P T and with more time given to French. Scripture made a specialist subject, English given by each Form Master. Nature and Technical Drawing introduced in form 1. School morning assembly was begun as a regular part of the school day.

4th March 1949

Mrs R Jones reported for duty as Clerical Assistant.

28th March 1949

The following boys were successful in their exams and will be transferred to Technical College: M J Brimsden, K Brittain, B Brown, B J Chapman, C Gibson, G R Grange, L Hartley, R Insley, T Middleton, R Naylor, J W Pratt, Bryan Snelson, N Shackleton, Dennis Wales.

2nd April 1949

The swimming teams competed in the Schools' competition for the "Grimsby Cup" with the A team winning and the B team runners up.

Two teams competed in the Drama classes at Grimsby Musical Festival and won 1st and 2nd Prize for short plays.

8th May 1949

Mr Dearden left to take up an appointment as Headmaster, Holme Hill Junior School.

Mr D A Nowell slipped from a ladder whilst preparing for a lantern lecture in the Girls' Dept. and was taken to hospital for treatment.

Sports Day on the boulevard

12th May 1949

The school was closed for the day due to Municipal Elections.

Brian Snelson was successful in gaining a scholarship at Wintringham Grammar School.

There are now 613 boys on the register.

Two Union Jubilee 5 inch centre woodworking lathes costing £226 -14-0 were placed in the Woodwork Dept.

Mr A H Wardley joined the staff from Holme Hill School and Mr D M Gregory as an assistant Master.

2nd June 1949

The school athletic sports meeting was held on Boulevard Recreation ground. The weather was fine and was a very successful venture.

9th June 1949

From 1.30pm till 4.00pm the school was opened to parents. A large number estimated at 200 visited the school during the afternoon. A display of camping was held on the lawn. Displays of boxing, Physical Training and games were also held on the lawn and in the Hall, two short plays were performed on the lawn whilst in the classrooms work was exhibited alongside lessons in woodwork, Art and Science.

13th June 1949

24 boys under Messrs Lee and Dixon left by bus for a week's camp at Stratford upon Avon with visits to places of historical interest and to the Shakespeares Memorial Theatre. On their return a second party of boys under Messrs Nowell and Hollingsworth took over the camp.

27th June 1949

Mr S Marchant joined the staff as an assistant master.

30th June - 7th July 1949

A party of boys under messrs Withers and Marlborough went on a weeks visit to Paris and Versailles

13th July 1949

The school was closed all day for the Duke of Edinburgh's visit to Grimsby.

5th Sept 1949

There was 741 on the register at start of term

26th Sept 1949

The Staff Football Team played the A team on the Paper Mills ground, Littlefield Lane at 4.15pm. A good crowd gathered to watch the Staff win by 8 goals to 4 and over £8 was raised for school funds.

22nd Nov 1949

40 boys from form 3a attended a lecture on ballet in the Girls' School.

3rd Dec 1949

The A Football Team defeated Welholme School in the final of the Roberts Cup by 4 goals to 1, thus retaining the cup for the second year.

1950

16th Jan 1950

School re-opened with 664 on register. In place of the "Leaver's Form" V, a new form was created in Form 1 to be called 1x and placed under Mr Nowell. The average number in each class shows a considerable reduction, the highest being 44 and the lowest 32. In the timetable 3 lessons each week were allotted to 3B to undertake some project work.

21st Feb 1950

School closed all day for General Elections.

15th March 1950

The school Swimming Gala was held at Orwell St. Baths at 7.00pm all seats were filled by parents and friends. The programme worked smoothly, competition was keen and enthusiasm high and a very successful evening was enjoyed.

30th March 1950

The following boys were offered places at the Technical school as a result of their recent exams:

Technical: Stanley Havercroft, Roger R Howard, Ewan W Lond, Terry Pascoe, Geoffrey Peers, Peter Turner, Barry Thurston, Ronald E Thompson.

Commercial: Brian Evans, George W Proctor, David Rudd, Colin S Swinborne

Building Exams: Brian Hames, Sydney Hargitt, Peter Hufton, Brian C Parkinson, Barry Woodward.

2nd April 1950

School reopened with 601 boys on the register. New radiators were fitted in rooms 3&4 and upstairs workshop.

1st May 1950

24 boys with Mr Withers and Mr Marlborough left for Paris at midday.

Mr Lee and Mr Dixon took a party of boys for a week's camp at Stratford upon Avon

20th May 1950

A second party left for Stratford upon Avon with Mr Hollingsworth and Mr Nowell.

9th June 1950

The school athletic Sports Day was held at Clee Fields from 2.00pm till 4.00pm. The boys were carried in buses at a charge of two pence each journey. The weather proved fine and the meeting was successful.

22nd June 1950

The school was opened to parents in the afternoon session. The Hall was set out with a display of woodwork models, handicrafts, trophies, art and project work

3rd July 1950

Mr H Spicker reported for duty as an assistant master.

6th July 1950

The school was closed for the Inter Schools Sports at Clee Fields. The school won the trophy again by a comfortable margin.

13th July 1950

The school A swimming team won the Maddock Cup and Hewitt Shield in record times at the Inter Schools swimming Gala.

24rd July 1950

A party of 30 boys under Mr Coleman and Mr Herbert will leave for a 3-day visit to Portsmouth and London. They will stay on H M S Victoria and Albert, have a tour of the Dockyard and visit London on return.

4th Sept 1950

The number of new boys enrolled was 177 making a grand total of 701 boys on register with 18 classes.

New members of staff were **Mr B S Smith, Mr L O Peters, Mr L Walker,** and **Mr H Spicker.**

Mr Hayes was transferred to Scarthoe School and Mr Forde left to take up a post with Home Office.

FORM	TEACHER	NO OF BOYS
5	Mr Nowell	43
4a	Mr Lee	33
4b	Mr Dixon	42
4c	Mr Goulding	42
4d	Mr Wardley	38
3a	Mr Hollingsworth	36
3b	Mr Leake	44
3c	Mr Fox	41
3d	Mr Walker	38
2a	Mr Withers	42
2b	Mr Holmes	45
2c	Mr Hotchkin	44
2d	Mr Peters	43
1a	Mr Abe	42
1b1	Mr Marchant	35
1b2	Mr Spicker	31
1c	Mr Herbert	32
1d	Mr Coleman	30
-	Mr Gregory	
-	Mr B Smith	

26th Sept 1950

The school swimming team won the Coulbeck & Dyas Trophies at Orwell St. Baths.

29th Sept 1950

The school was closed at 3.30pm to enable all boys and masters to attend the Staff v Boys football match at Dixon's Paper Mills ground. The staff won by 8 goals to 1. A good crowd assembled and the sum of £8 -6-0 was raised for the schools fund.

24th Nov 1950

At the Inter Schools Swimming Gala the school team won the Telegraph Shield, the Acklam Cup and the Holder Cup.

9th Dec 1950

The school 11 defeated Welholme School by 2 goals to 1 to retain the Roberts Trophy for the third successive year.

14th Dec 1950

An end of term concert was given in the school Hall on separate afternoons for pupils and parents. Two plays produced by Mr Spicker and Mr Wardley and items by a choir under Mr Walker completed the programme.

1951

28th Feb 1951

The school swimming gala was held at Orwell St. Baths at 7.00pm. The Hall was filled to capacity with boys, parents and friends. The swimming was of a very high standard, the competition and enthusiasm very keen. Mr Lee was responsible for the organisation, which worked very smoothly. A very successful evening.

16th March 1951

School swimming team retained the Hewitt Shield in the record time of 1.59 at the Inter Schools Gala.

A play produced by Mr Spicker, was given as a radio play in the Hall, "The Kings Supper" an extract from "The man born to be King", this proved an exacting task for the boys, and the part of Jesus was taken by D Taylor.

17th April 1951

School re-opened with 601 boys on the register.

1st June 1951

The school sports were held at Clee Fields at 2.15pm, the boys being moved by private bus.

14th June 1951

The school was opened to parents in the afternoon. Displays of work were arranged in each room, while in the Hall an exhibition of woodwork models, art handicrafts, project work and trophies were arranged. On the Quad displays of P T, boxing and a play entitled "Noah's Flood" was presented. The weather kept fine and a large number of visitors came to the school. The Headmaster entertained the staff and friends to tea in the Staff Room.

18th June 1951

24 boys under Mr Lee and Mr Dixon left by coach for Stratford upon Avon where they will camp until Saturday.

27th June 1951

The following boys were awarded places at Technical College:

John Benton, George Burnett, Ronald Creathorne, Harry de St Croix, Joseph Desforges, Craig Lill, Gordon Needham, George Tywell, Peter Wheatley.

7th July 1951

The school swimming team retained the Telegraph Shield in competition and created a new record in winning the Acklam Cup.

12th July 1951

School was closed for the inter school sports when the Championship Trophy was retained for the fifth year in succession.

10th Sept 1951

School opened at 9.15am. There was a new entry of 187 boys from Primary schools with 7 others making the full total 725 boys. The organisation was as follows:

FORM	TEACHER	NO OF BOYS
1d	Mr Coleman	36
1c	Mr J M Gregory	36
1b2	Mr A Hopkinson	35
1b1	Mr H Spicker	40
1a	Mr H Abe	42
2d	Mr L Peters	42
2c	Mr D Hotchkin	42
2b	Mr M Holmes	42
2a	Mr A Withers	39
3d	Mr K Walker	42
3c	Mr R Fox B A	44
3b	Mr A Leake	44
3a	Mr W Hollingsworth	44
4d	Mr A Wardley	39
4c	Mr H Goulding	39
4b	Mr G Dixon	42
4a	Mr A Lee	35
5	Mr D Nowell	43
-	Mr C Herbert	
-	Mr B Smith	
-	Mr G Marlborough	
-	Mr J Armstrong	

Mr S Marchant left to take up an appointment in Nigeria with **Mr Hopkinson** replacing him.

Slight adjustments of curriculum have been made; shorthand has now been completely dropped. Technical Drawing is taken in 4A to complete a four-year course. Gardening is to be supplemented in the "B" stream by a course in Nature Study and Biology.

Mrs. Cleave of the Child Guidance Service will attend the school in afternoon sessions for remedial work.

2nd Oct 1951

The school swimming team retained the Coulbeck Cup.

5th Dec 1951

The school swimming team retained the Maddock Cup at the schools swimming gala at Orwell St. Baths with a new record of 1.59 minutes.

11th Dec 1951

A party of boys went to watch an exhibition in South Parade School by Randolph Turpin, World Boxing Champion.

A school concert called "The Bishops Candlesticks" and "The Golden West" and musical items by the school choir was given in the Hall each day and to parents and visitors on Thursday

1952

15th Jan 1952

Mr A B Leake left the staff being transferred to Elliston St. School. There are 664 boys on register, divided into 17 classes.

31st Jan 1952

A party from the school gave a concert at St. Marks, Nunsthorpe for church funds.

15th Feb 1952

A special assembly was held at 2.00pm as a memorial service for the death of His Majesty King George VI. Two minute's silence was observed.

Frank Chase was transferred to Carr Lane Academic Stream and the following boys were successful at Technical:

Derek Keeton, John Sizer, Gordon Booth, Thomas Cook, Roy Foxon, Roland Hotson, Frank Maddison, Peter Rex, Alfred Simpson, Anthony Tyler, Michael Waumsley, Keith Young, George Camplin, Neil Cooper, Roland Hill, Arthur Hoyle, David Plowright, John Ritchie, Donald Sandvig, Peter Walker, James Woodhouse.

24th March 1952

The school swimming team retained the Hewitt Shield at School Swimming Sports with K Brockelsby winning the School Championship Cup.

5th April 1952

The School Drama Team competed in the Grimsby Musical Festival with their play "The Golden West" under Mr Spicker. They won 1st prize in the under 16 class and second in the competition for the Caxton Cup.

29th April 1952

Mr C A Coleman left to take up an appointment of Headship and has been replaced by Mr J K Wignall, who will take over 1d.

5th June 1952

24 boys under Messr. Lee and Dixon left for a week's camp at Stratford upon Avon followed the following week by a party led by Mr Nowell and Mr Hollingsworth.

3rd July 1952

The school was closed for the Interschool Sports Day and the Grimsby News Trophy was retained for the eighth time in nine years.

7th July 1952

Mr D Holah joined the staff.

10th July 1952

The school was thrown open to parents in the afternoon. Classrooms were suitably prepared, an exhibition of work given in the Hall and a play, "The King's Warrant", produced by Mr Spicker was given on the Quad. Displays of P T followed. There was a very large attendance of visitors. The Headmaster and his wife entertained the staff to tea.

14th July 1952

Mr G Holley and Mr Hoose joined the staff.

18th July 1952

The swimming team retained the Telegraph Shield and the Acklam Cup.

8th Sept 1952

The September Term had a total of 686 boys and the organisation was as follows:

FORM	TEACHER	NO OF BOYS
1d	Mr J K Wignall	34
1c	Mr H Spicker	38
1b	Mr A Hopkinson	42
1a	Mr H Abe	42
2d	Mr L Peters	25
2c1	Mr G Holley	26
2c2	Mr D Hotchkin	43
2b	Mr M Holmes	43
2a	Mr H Withers	44
3d	Mr K Walker	40
3c	Mr R Fox B A	42
3b	Mr L R Hoose	41
3a	Mr W Hollingsworth	32
4d	Mr D Holah	42
4c	Mr H Goulding	43
4b	Mr G Dixon	42
4a	Mr Lee	35
5	Mr Nowell	32
-	Mr C Herbert	
-	Mr B Smith	
-	Mr A Wardley	
-	Mr G Marlborough	
-	Mr J Armstrong	

1st Nov 1952

Mr C Herbert was transferred to Nunsthorpe Primary school and was replaced by Mr D Wilkinson who joined the staff on 1 Nov.

1953

March 1953

As a result of the recent examinations the following boys have been selected for transfer to Grammer and Technical streams at 12+ years:

Grammer : Colin Stubbs, Derek Lusby, Brian Ward.

Technical Commercial : John Comins, Gordon S Dine, Alistair Russell, Anthony Scarborough.

Technical Engineering: Jas Atkinson, Geoffrey Bell, Stanley Brittain, Roger Cable, Barry Cox, Michael Ellis, Dave Gibbs, Roy Harrison, David Johnson, William Longbottom, Anthony Maddison, Kenneth Mann, Byron Marriott, Ewan Mitchell, David Pougher, John Radley, Eric Saville, Brian Smith, Phillip Smith, Brian Swinburne, Terence Swinburne, Brian Wright, Allan Vessey.

21st March 1953

The school cross country team won the Grimsby Harriers Cross Country Cup at the annual race at Scartho. Roy Lawrence won the individual championship.

28th April 1953

During the holidays a party of 20 boys under Messrs Hollingsworth, Fox and Marlborough stayed near Keswick and completed a week's walking holiday in the Lake District.

Mr L Peters left to take up duty at Woodhall Spa.

School teams entered a Road Safety Cycle Competition and won both Senior and Junior Trophies.

29th May - 4th June 1953

The school was closed until 4th June for the Coronation holiday.

4th June 1953

A tea party was held in both Boys & Girls Schools for the Coronation.

5th June 1953

The whole school was moved by Corporation buses at 2.00pm to Clee Fields. The weather was cold but fine and all events were completed with "Tennyson House" winning the championship.

15th June 1953

24 boys under Mr Lee and Mr Dixon left for Stratford upon Avon at 9.15am to camp until Saturday.

18th June 1953

The school was given permission to attend the "Gaumont" Cinema at 10.15am to see the Coronation film "A Queen is crowned".

20th June 1953

Mr Hollingsworth and Mr Nowell took the second party camping to Stratford.

9th July 1953

School was closed for the InterSchool Sports Day. The Grimsby News Trophy was retained for the ninth successive time.

16th July 1953

The school was opened to parents and visitors; the Girls school was also open. Classrooms were suitably prepared, an exhibition of work was held in the Hall and in the Girls' Hall. A pageant "Great Elizabeth", scenes from the times of Elizabeth I, was given on the Quadrangle. The items included Country Dancing, recorder playing and singing by girls in costume with games, sport and two extracts from King Henry V by the boys. There was a very large attendance of parents and friends. The Staff were entertained to tea by the Headmaster.

9th Sept 1953

School was opened at 9.15am. There was an intake of 148 boys bringing the school total to 634 boys.

The organisation is as follows:

FORM	TEACHER	NO OF BOYS
1d	Mr Smith	23
1c	Mr Hoose	32
1b	Mr Holley	23
1a2	Mr Holmes	32
1a1	Mr Abe	32
2d	Mr Wilkinson	29
2c	Mr Holah	40
2b	Mr Hotchkin	36
2a	Mr Spicker	43
3d	Mr Walker	34
3c	Mr Hopkinson	39
3b	Mr Lee	39
3a	Mr Hollingsworth	39
4d	Mr Withers	36
4c	Mr Goulding	40
4b	Mr Dixon	40
4a	Mr Fox	29
5	Mr Nowell	41
-	Mr Armstrong	
-	Mr Boyson	
-	Mr Wignall	
-	Mr Wheeler (part time)	
-	Mrs Cleave	

Mr Wardley left and has been replaced by Mr C R Boyson.

23rd Sept 1953

The School Dentist visited Watkin St. Clinic where all classes were examined.

15th Oct 1953

The School Drama Team under Mr H Spicker won first place in the Drama Competition at Bradley Musical Festival.

15th Dec 1953

A Drama festival in which each class enacted a play entirely unassisted by the staff was held on four days this week. Each form made a good effort, costume expertise being extremely noteworthy and in some cases the plays were very happily chosen. The winners were 4a with the radio play "The Cruel Sea"; 3b with "Alfred burnt the cakes"; 2a with "Hadrian's Wall"; and 1b2 with Robin Hood and the Bishop of Arlington.

1954

12th Jan 1954

There were 584 boys on the register. With Mr L Hoose and Mr Wignall having left, some reorganisation was necessary with Mr Holley taking over 1C

1st Feb 1954

The 1st year attended a concert given in the central Hall by the new English Symphony Orchestra.

The school drama team presented "Hadrian's Wall" at the festival at Clee Grammar School and were highly commended by the adjudicators.

15th March 1954

The school swimming gala was held at Orwell St. Baths. The house cup was won by Newton House and the individual cup by Smith.

At an assembly in the Hall, John Hough was presented with a Silver medal by the Dumb Friends League for rescuing two dogs from the sea at Cleethorpes.

3rd May 1954

There were 535 boys on register. The following boys have been awarded places at the Technical College in September: P Abbott, L Barber, D Chapman, G Dolby, W Forrester, M Foster, R Hinch, A Houltby, D Parker, F Patrick, S Redding, P Richman, R Swift, A Waumsley, A Wolfe, E Aldred.

14th June 1954

A party of 24 boys under Mr Lee and Mr Dixon left for camp at Stratford upon Avon.

19th June 1954

A second party left under Mr Nowell and Hollingsworth to camp.

22nd June 1954

Boys from the second, third and fourth year were taken to the Chest Clinic for X ray.

8th July 1954

The school team came second in the Inter School Sports to Carr Lane by a narrow margin, so lost the Grimsby News Trophy which they had won 9 times in 10 years. 3 boys, Swain, Stubbs and Harrison set new records.

15th July 1954

The school was opened to parents in the afternoon session. Each classroom had an arrangement of its own work while an exhibition of woodcraft work, art and technical drawing was held in the Hall. Displays of P T under Messrs Holmes and Holley were given on the lawn and a play **"Pioneers of Pioneers"** performed by 3a under Mr Spicker. There were many hundreds of visitors. The Headmaster entertained staff and guests to tea.

The cast from 3a were: Thomas Cook, Carl Rushby, Anthony Smith, Michael Cator, Kenneth Margraves, Kenneth Pacey, Martin Campbell, Ronald Scrimshaw, Brian Jackson, Roger Dunton.

Allocations of Special posts for 1955/56 were noted in the Education Committee notes as:

ASSISTANT	GIRLS	BOYS
1st	Miss P Disney	Mr A Lee
2nd	Mrs G Brook	Mr D A Nowell
3rd	Miss J H Shaw	Mr H Abe
4th	Miss C Harvey	Mr A H Goulding
5th	Mrs J Partridge	Mr A H Withers
6th		Mr G R Dixon

© Grimsby Telegraph

Pioneers of Pioneers performed at School open day.

During the holidays the school interior woodwork has been painted and repairs carried out on the lavatory roof and window sills. In the huts changes have been made to the interior structure so that room 14 was enlarged by the addition of store room space and a fitted sink. This will be used for art. Room 15 was enlarged by taking in the classrooms at each end; a new storeroom has been added. This is to be used as a workshop when the equipment is provided. Room 16 was enlarged by taking in the cloakroom and will be used for Technical Drawing. Rooms 17 and 18 have been joined into one large room and a store provided.

The Chapman St premises formerly used as a kitchen has been cleared out and prepared for use for PT.

School was opened with 587 boys on register.

7th Sept 1954

Mr T J Chadwick joined the staff as an assistant master to teach Science and Games.

20th Sept 1954

The School Medical Officer has made a series of visits to give a Tuberculosis vaccine.

21st Oct 1954

The Drama Team won the competition at Bradley Festival with "Pioneers of Pioneers". The Cup was retained for the second year. The Team and Mr Spicker were highly commended by the adjudicator.

24th Nov 1954

Attendance began to drop due to an epidemic of influenza. 162 absent with the following week had risen to 184 absent.

December 1954

A blackout room was granted to the Girls' school for use of projector.

21st Dec 1954

The school Prize Giving for 1953-54 and a Carol Service was conducted in the Hall by the Chairman of the School Governors, Mr G A Pearson.

Armstrong St. Boy's School Teaching Staff 1954

Geoff Boyson, Graham Holley, Trevor Chadwick, Don Hotchkin, Derek Wilkinson,
Harold Spicker, Dennis Holah, Bernard Smith, Ken Walker

Max Holmes, Ron Fox, Harry Abe, Reg Dixon, John Holmes (Headmaster), Alf Lee,
David Nowell, Alec Withers, Geoff Malborough, Bill Hollingsworth

1955

School reopened with 632 boys on register.

A potter's wheel was obtained for the craft section together with provision of bicycle stands. Electric lighting was installed in the Boys' & Girls' toilets. Fluorescent lighting was installed in the Girls' Needlework Room.

3rd Feb 1955

A party of 36 boys attended a concert by the London Philharmonic Orchestra in the Central Hall.

15th Feb 1955

A garden shed on the school allotments has been completed and is in use as a store and shelter.

The shelves in the storeroom next to the Headmaster's room have been removed and transferred to the small store opposite, formerly used as a wood store. This gives a useful room for medical inspections, interviews and the remedial teacher.

16th Feb 1955

Workmen have begun excavating some foundations of the school Hall for the Engineers' report on Subsidence.

An invited audience of parents were shown the play "Scuttlebooms Treasure" and in the Drama Festival held at Clee Grammer School on 11th March it was very highly commended. The cast were as follows:

Rosebud . . . . Robert Young
Red Bill . . . . Carl Rushby
Sharkey Joe . . . . Bernard Briggs
Jamaica Jim . . . . William Perry
Black Joe . . . . Robert Macdonald
Slimey Pete . . . . Dave Rushby
Look-out man . . . . Kenneth Pacey
Titterton . . . . Robert Bemrose
Cutlass . . . . Terence Howes
One eye . . . . John Heath
Ebenezer Scuttleboom . Michael Cator
T Aloysuis Fish . . . . Thomas Cook
Jones . . . . Martin Campbell

Other members of cast: John Collier, Kenneth Sissons, Stephen Bessant, Ronald May, Peter Thorton, Malcolm Anderson, Kenneth Wilcox

Producer: Mr H Spicker

The school swimming sports were held at Orwell St. Baths. P R Addison won the individual championship and Newton House won the Horn Cup.

The following boys have been selected for transfer to the Technical College:

Martin Campbell, Brian Jackson Ronald May Cyril Robinson, Thomas Cook, John Cowell, John Cuthbertson, Roger Dunton, Brian Fixter, Roland Gibbons, Kenneth Harrison, George Havercroft, Alan Holton, Robert McDonald, Brian Money, Kenneth Sisson, Anthony Smith, Carl Poole, Geoffrey Roberts, Harold Taylor, Eric Thornley, Barry Thirtle, David Walker

13th June 1955

24 boys under Messrs Nowell and Hollingsworth went to Stratford upon Avon by motor coach to a week's camp.

23rd June 1955

A school team of four took part in a Safety First Quiz against a team from St. James' School and were defeated by two points.

30th June 1955

The school speech day and prize giving was held in the Town Hall which was filled to capacity with boys and parents. The prizes were distributed by Professor G Mayfield of the University of Hull who was guest speaker.

Mr A Hopkinson left the staff at the end of summer term to take an appointment on the Isle of Wight.

During the holiday a party of boys were taken to H M Dockyard, Chatham by Messrs Holley and Wilkinson for a four-day stay.

Sept 1955

There are 512 boys on the register divided into 16 classes. The first year intake of 110 was divided into two instead of the usual 4 streams. A fifth year class of Christmas leavers was created with two sections in 4a, the newly promoted section of 4th year doing more advanced work.

During the holiday redecoration in pastel shades had been carried out in the huts giving a clean and pleasing effect.

It was not possible to begin Metalwork, although all the necessary equipment has arrived, because no suitable teacher could be recruited.

21st Sept 1955

A quartet of musicians of the New English Orchestra gave an hour's concert to the boys and girls of Form 2 in the School Hall.

1956

25th Jan 1956

The School Dramatic Society performed the two plays "Spring comes to Diamondo" & "King Arthur and the Cakes" at Old Clee School in the Grimsby Schools Drama Festival.

22nd Feb 1956

Cricket nets were installed in Chapman St. and new gym benches delivered.

13th March 1956

An incident occurred in school between a Master, Mr Hotchkin, who was struck by the parent of Ray Phillips, 2d, during break. On the 19th March Mr Phillips attended school and signed an apology admitting liability and expressing his regret.

17th April 1956

During Easter break, wall bars were fitted to Chapman St. Gym and a new vaulting box delivered. The forge in the Metal Workshop was placed in position and chimney attached.

There are 436 boys on the register.

24th April 1956

31 boys were transferred to Technical: R Appleton, J Blendell, C Brown, R Bridges, G Bunn, L Burns, G Burrage, W Blow, D Crockart, B Curtis, S Draycott, A Ellis, D Everett, L Fairfield, B Fanthorpe, M Giles, E Hewson, D Hudson, C Iverson, C Lee, T Lowbridge, R Marsh, G Metcalfe, M Payne B Perkins L Pigg, R Pull, T Robinson, T Scott, E Thompson and P Thorton.

P Shepherd to Carr Lane Grammar.

30th April 1956

Mr Holmes relinquished the Headship to take over the Headship of Beacon Hill School, Cleethorpes.

1st May 1956

I, Alfred L Lee became Master in charge until the appointment of a new Headmaster.

1st June 1956

In the afternoon the whole school went by bus to Clee Fields for Sports Day. The Horn Cup for athletics was won by Franklin House.

11-16th June 1956

26 boys in charge of Messrs Nowell and Hollingsworth were at camp at Stratford upon Avon. A full programme of visits and activities was carried out.

27th June 1956

The Annual Speech Day & Prizegiving was held in the Town Hall. The prizes were presented by Mr J Holmes, to whom a brief-case was presented by the boys and a silver salver by the staff to mark his seven years work as Headmaster of the school. Mr Holmes presented to the school a silver cup to be awarded annually to the boy who had contributed most in service and example to the school.

27th July 1956

School closed for the Summer holiday. Messrs Fox, Spicker, Wilkinson and Boyson left to take up appointments at other schools During the first week of the holidays, 30 boys in charge of Messrs Hotchkin and Holah were on a visit to Chatham Dockyard.

1st Sept 1956

I, Alfred Lee, was appointed Headmaster with effect from 1st Sept 1956. The staff as follows:

Mr A L Lee (Headmaster)	21-3-1898
Mr J N Armstrong	25-3-1913
Mr D A Nowell (Deputy)	10-3-1900
Mr D A Hotchkin	19-11-1916
Mr H Abe	4-8-1906
Mr B S Smith	21-11-1912
Mr A Withers	19-11-1898
Mr K A Walker	15-11 1923
Mr H Goulding	7-11-1905
Mr G Holley	28-6-1930
Mr G R Dixon	22-7-1908
Mr J D Holah	22-4-1930
Mr M M Holmes	24-12-1908
Mr J T Chadwick	6-11-1931
Mr G F Marlborough	26-9-1910
Mr W D Hollingsworth	1-11-1909
Mr W C Towle (part-time)	
Mr J Wheeler (part-time)	
Mrs. E T Cleave (part-time)	

Armstrong St School Staff 1956

Back: Ken Walker, Harry Abe, Alec Withers, Don Hotchkin, Dennis Holah, Graham Holley, Trevor Chadwick, Bill Hollingsworth – Seated: Max Holmes, Bernard Smith, John Armstrong, David Nowell, Alfred Lee, Mrs P Woods, Secretary, Reg Dixon, Geoff Marlborough, Harry Goulding

Sept 1956

Cracks in the structure of the school had increased recently and during the holidays half of the Hall has been sealed off. It is possible to accommodate only three or four classes in the half left in use and morning assembly is taken with each year in turn over the week.

Smaller numbers in the school and depletion of staff have made necessary the re-organisation from four streams to three. There are 440 boys in 13 classes, 3 forms to each year with the addition of a fifth form of 32 boys who have completed the fourth year course but are unable to leave until Christmas.

Mr Towle, a retired metalwork teacher has agreed to return to teaching for two and a half days weekly.

1st October 1956

Recommendations by Education Authority of titles and responsibilities:

- Mr D A Nowell Deputy Head Teacher
- Mr H Abe Head of the English Dept.
- Mr G R Dixon Head of Mathematics Dept.
- Mr A Withers
- Mr G Holley the care, maintenance & ordering of Physical Education equipment
- Mr W Hollingsworth Geography, History throughout the school
- Mr D A Hotchkin Technical Drawing

1957

8th Jan 1957

There are 407 boys on the register including 10 who could have left at Christmas. The staff is unchanged.

20th March 1957

The whole of the second year attended an orchestral concert at the Town Hall in the afternoon.

Armstrong Boys Road Safety Quiz team won the finals trophy at the Town Hall. The team consisted of Brian Nuttell, Dave Nundy, Michael Shepherd(Capt) and Fred Tartellin.

27th June 1957

School Speech Day at Town Hall. Mr Roderick Bennett J P presented the prizes.

10th Sept 1957

The school opened the new term with 442 boys on the register. Mr Towle has agreed to teach Metalwork full time, a generous gesture, which will be of the greatest value to the school.

The staff has been augmented by Mr Michael Woods (28.1.35) from Sheffield Training College.

Attendance has dropped through the last week each day as influenza spreads. Average for the week 78%. The following week was 64%.

11th Oct 1957

Attendance back up to 90% as the worst of the epidemic is over.

1958

7th Jan 1958

School reopened with 415 boys on register. Mrs M Franklin took over the duties of School Secretary, Mrs P Woods having retired due to illness.

13th March 1958

The second year forms attended a concert by the New England Orchestra at Chelmsford School.

4th June 1958

The annnual Sports Day for the school was held on Clee Fields this afternoon.

16th June 1958

26 boys in charge of Messrs Nowell and Hollingsworth left today for a six day school camp at Stratford upon Avon.

3rd July 1958

The annual Speech Day was held in the Town Hall in the afternoon.The Mayor, Alderman M Larmour presented the prizes.

7th July 1958

Mr D Shaw joined the staff.

9th Sept 1958

465 boys were on the register with Mr J Wheeler, the music teacher leaving and Mr D Shaw joining the staff.

1959

7th Jan 1959

There are 443 boys on the register.

16th March 1959

A Dinner/Dance for fourth and fifth year boys and girls was held at the Winter Gardens, Cleethorpes.

20th March 1959

The school road safety team was chosen to represent Grimsby in an inter towns contest at Louth with the team winning the Challenge Shield.

The annual Swimming Gala was held at Orwell St Baths in the evening, The Horn swimming Cup was won by Tennyson House.

27th May 1959

The annual Athletics Sports were held on Clee Fields in the afternoon. The Horn Athletics Cup was won by Hereward House.

8th June 1959

40 boys went to the YMCA hutted camp at Humberstone for a week of outdoor studies. The boys were in the charge of Mr Holah and Mr Wood.

25th June 1959

Speech Day was held in the Town Hall in the afternoon. The prizes were presented by Mr John Bennett, the managing Director of Northern Trawlers.

29th June 1959

26 boys with Mr Nowell and Mr Hollingsworth went by motor coach to a week's camp at Tootles, Hants.

1st July 1959

The first boys in this school to sit for the G C E Exams took metalwork exam today. Seven boys are sitting four subjects each.

7th Sept 1959

The school opened with 482 boys on the register with Mr W McCrohan joining the staff from Victoria Jun. Boys' School.

YMCA Camp at Humberstone

Armstrong St. Boy's School Teaching Staff 1960

Back: Keith Turner, Graham Holley, Trevor Chadwick, M Wood, Bernard Smith, Hugh M Crohan, Dennis Holah, Ken Walker, L Driver
Front: Alec Withers, Walter C Towle, Bill Hollingsworth, Reg Dixon, David Nowell, Alf Lee (Headmaster),
Mrs Sanderson, Secretary, Harry Abe, Max Holmes, Geoff Marlborough, Don Hotchkin

Oct 1959

The results of the GCE Exams previously taken by seven boys were: one boy passed in 3 subjects, 2 boys passed in 2 subjects and 2 boys passed in 1 subject.

Mr Withers has returned to school after an illness, which began in May.

1960

5th Jan 1960

School reopened with 454 boys.

6th May 1960

School closed today for Princess Margaret's Wedding.

12th May 1960

School closed due to being used as a Polling Booth.

13th June 1960

36 boys and 2 Masters went to YMCA camp at Humberstone for the week. A course of work chiefly nature study and surveying is being done based on the facilities afforded by the area.

22nd June 1960

The annual school mile race was run on the Boulevard this afternoon.

30th June 1960

The school has been reassessed as an examination centre by the Cambridge Examinations syndicate and 13 boys began their G C E exams. 10 boys taking 5 subjects each and 3 boys, 4 subjects each.

7th July 1960

Speech Day was held in the Town Hall this afternoon, the prizes being presented by Col. J Wintringham.

6th Sept 1960

School reopened with 453 boys on the register. Mr Towle is now working 3 days per week and Mr K Turner, who was attached as an extra Handicraft Teacher has remained on the staff. The school has been repainted inside during the holidays using lighter and brighter colours than previously - the present improvement most noticeable.

19th Dec 1960

The Annual Dinner/Dance held conjointly with the Girls' School took place in the evening at the Winter Gardens.

1961

10th Jan 1961

School reopened with 423 boys on register.

22nd June 1961

Speech Day was held at the Town Hall. Mr Graham Cann presented the prizes.

17th July 1961

Form 3c are at the YMCA camp at Humberstone until 21st July .

25th July 1961

School Open Day.

12th Sept 1961

School reopened with 420 boys on register with a staff of 20. Mr J Blackburn taking Mr Woods place.

The results of the July GCE exams again show a marked advance. 12 boys were entered. 3 boys passed in 5 subjects, 4 boys in 4 subjects, and 5 boys in 3 subjects.

English 6 passes out of 12, Maths 11 out of 12, Technical Drawing 12 out of 12, Metalwork 12 out of 12, Woodwork 4 out of 4.

1962

9th Jan 1962

School reopened with 385 boys on register.

1st May 1962

School reopened with 354 boys on the register.

21st June 1962

Speech Day took place in the Town Hall with Mr P Appleyard presenting the prizes.

16th July 1962

28 boys in charge of Messrs Hotchkin and Holah left for camp at Botley, Hants. until 21st July.

27th July 1962

School closed for summer holiday and I, Alfred L Lee today relinquished the Headship, on retirement.

Sept 1962

The school opened with 367 boys with Mr J Evison and Mr A Sharp joined the staff.

I, **George Reginald Dixon**, was appointed acting Headmaster with effect from 1st Sept. 1962.

Armstrong St School Staff 1961

Back: Graham Holley, Trevor Chadwick, M Wood, Bernard Smith, Alec Withers, Ken Walker, Dennis Holah
Seated: Don Hotchkin, Walter Towle, Reg Dixon, Dan Nowell, Alf Lee, Harry Abe, Geoff Marlborough, Max Holmes, Bill Hollingsworth

The following appointments were also made,

- **Mr H Abe** Acting Deputy Headmaster
- **Mr D Hotchkin** Departmental Head –Mathematics
- **Mr H A Withers** Departmental Head – English
- **Mr G F Marlborough** Post for Technical Drawing

The school is divided into 3 streams in each year.

Miss Ann Pettit took over the duties as School Secretary.

Mr D A Nowell has returned 2½ days per week to teach Science.

Mr A Sharp started as temp. teacher.

1963

9th May 1963

School closed for Municipal Elections. School used as Polling Station.

15th July 1963

28 boys and two Masters spent a week camping at Botley on Southampton waters.

Mr D H Armstrong joined the staff as Assistant Master.

26 July 1963

Mr W C Towle and Mr B Elvin resigned. Mr B Smith was transferred to Chelmsford Boys.

30th July 1963

Boilers in 3 huts replaced at a cost of £670.

School Leavers Job Study

Remaining at school to take GCE O levels	14
Transferred to Technical College GCE A level	2
Skilled apprenticeships	31
Clerical	2
Factory Workers	1
Sawmill workers	2
Shop Assistants	2
Misc	3
Fishing Industry	2

10th Sept 1963

The following members joined the staff: Mr N Robinson (Music), Mr K Tappin (PE & Maths), Mr A Sapcote (Science) and Miss L Pickering (Maths).

Nov 1963

Visits were planned for Fisons, Lloyds Cars, Dixon's Paper Mills and Dunlop.

17th Dec 1963

Joint Dinner-Dance at the Winter Gardens with the Girls' School.

18th Dec 1963

Inter House Basketball Competition.

19th Dec 1963

Carol Service in School Hall.

1964

15th Jan 1964

Visit to Doig's shipyard for launching of vessel.

15-20th Jan 1964

Medicals and TB Tests.

21st Jan 1964

Visited Royal Navy Ship in Dock.

23rd Jan 1964

3rd year BCG inoculation.

28th Jan 1964

Sgt. J Buckley, Grimsby Borough Police, spoke to 4th year boys on the work of the police.

5th Feb 1964

Visit to Porter's Precision Tools work at Waltham.

12 Feb 1964

Soccer Inter House matches held at Clee Fields.

4a and 4b attended performance of opera "Don Pasquale" at Wintringham Boys' School.

23rd April 1964

Seven boys from form 5x visited
Fowlers Foundry with Mr Turner.

25th April 1964

Three staff (Messrs Holley, Tappin and
Sapcote) took a party of boys to London
to see England Boys v Germany, including
a coach tour of places of interest.

27th May 1964

Investigated charge of extorsion with
menaces from a pupil. Three pupils from 3b
class have admitted the offence and were
caned and ordered to make retribution.

4th June 1964

A joint Sport's Meeting with the
Girl's school was held on Clee
Fields but was spoiled by rain.

12th June 1964

Mr M Holmes took part in a cricket
coaching course at Western School.

26th June 1964

Cycling Awards made after assembly
by Coun. Shemwell, Chairman
of the Road Safety Council.

2nd July 1964

The School's last Speech Day and Prize
Giving were held in the Town Hall. Mr
J Rostron presenting the prizes.

21st July 1964

Mr Holley and Form 2b paid a visit to
Thornton Abbey for a historical lesson.

23rd July 1964

Removal vans started to move books
and equipment to Hereford School.

24th July 1964

The school closed its doors for the last time.

Signed, George R Dixon, Headmaster

*On the last day of school, Mr R Dixon told the assembled boys that the school was to be demolished
the following day by contractors, and so if they wished, on leaving school, they could break
the windows of the school. This offer to most boys was an obvious treat, yet not one boy on
leaving the school for the last time had the heart to throw a stone and deface their school.*

This chapter describes in detail the reports submitted by Headmasters and His Majesty's Inspectors during the school's reign.

General Test Report 1929

F B Potter 17th Dec 1929

A report on the first General Test in Reading, Arithmetic and English by the Headmaster.

The boys were assembled for the first time on September 30th, coming from the different schools, about 100 from St. Paul's, and 170 almost equally from South Parade Junior, and Lord Street, the first and last named being now closed.

The first classification – into 6 groups – was made on part knowledge and part recommendation. After 5 weeks, on Nov 5th, the lower 5 groups were split into 6, making 7 altogether. After a further 6 weeks or so this first test has been made and results recorded, as a consequence of which it may be found necessary to transfer a few boys still again.

Reading

In the upper half of the school reading is usually sufficiently fluent with creditable expression and phrasing, though articulation is not always good. Practice in the use of the dictionary is needed. Knowledge of Etymology is poor.

In the lower half there is a great variety, some exhibiting a profound ignorance of the very elements of speech and reading. Training in words –spelling, build, and meaning – has been neglected. Punctuation and phrasing is extraordinary, as also is the lack of general interest in the subject under consideration. This is reflected in other subjects, particularly singing.

English and Writing

Below the top class, which work at some length, the treatment of the subject of an essay is too scant; the horizon of ideas is too limited. Some in the lower classes seem at present rather hopeless, and will require constant help and guidance.

The writing of these classes is of necessity mixed and requires frequent practice. Spelling is not as good as it ought to be, and in some cases demands a regular, perhaps daily exercise.

The English knowledge of the top classes varies. Many boys know little of grammar and consequently are unable to detect and correct errors. The use of the pronoun in Composition is at fault. The Characteristics of Parts of Speech are strange to many. A detailed course of instruction should be planned for next term.

Beyond some carelessness in even copying words and punctuation, very few have had practice in answering a series of questions; spacing, headings, use of underlines, numbering or lettering, paragraphing, are all in need of careful instruction and insistence on exercise of attention to detail.

Arithmetic

The lower classes, 2 and 3, are generally well below standard. Whilst they are working squared paper, boys must be made to use the columns properly and uniformly, and to place sums on the paper neatly and according to instruction. As a rule sums should not be allowed to be placed side by side. Great progress is anticipated during next term.

The work of the upper classes is better, papers are neater, and accuracy is of a very fair standard. The work was marked more leniently than will be the case.

The present Std 4 must supply the scholarship boys for 1930. An early advance should be made to factors and multiples, fractions and decimals.

In general the older boys have settled down to ordered work and effort more quickly and successfully than the younger boys. Discipline is not as strict as expected. The greater the freedom allowed to boys, a feature to be cultivated in the future, particularly with older boys, the stricter must be the control.

Simultaneous recitation of anything should be avoided; it kills individual effort and style, and merely shelters the idle. Much of it in previous schools is reflected in the unpleasant, noisy chanting of morning prayers.

H M Inspectors' Report 1930

Inspected on 5-7th October 1930

Boy's Department

This school was opened on September 30th, 1929. The boys were drawn at first instance from St. Paul's Church of England and the Lord Street Temporary Council Schools (both now closed) and from the South Parade Council School. Since that date drafts have been received from Macaulay Street Church of England and Little Coates Council schools.

With one exception the assistant staff is distinctly capable; it contains experienced men who are bringing enthusiasm, and in several cases, specialised skill, to their work. Their notes and records are exceedingly well kept and show that they approach their work with very definite and well-considered aims. The plans for instruction have been set out in a very detailed syllabus, which, with the exception of English, may be regarded as generally suitable for the normal child. In English however, the work detailed in

Literature is of such an ambitious nature as to give the scheme the appearance of impracticability, so much of it entirely beyond the children's interest or comprehension.

Of the present roll of 383, approximately 160 boys are under eleven years of age. The organisation is in eight classes, of which four consist mainly of junior children. These four classes contain 43 senior boys, while 25 juniors are to be found in the senior classes. It will be seen that there is no "clean cut" at eleven years. Moreover, although three classes are described as of "B" attainments and contain boys of still lower mental grading, the curriculum pursued is the same as that for the normal children. The non-application of "Haddon" principles is ascribed by the Head Teacher to sundry reasons. On this point further consideration is highly desirable; it is quite certain that the school contains a large proportion of pupils who cannot follow the proposed course of instruction with any real success.

Among the more brightly endowed children there is a good deal that promises well. Much of the work is presented along appealing lines. The Arithmetic and Elementary Science are in close touch with actual life. Geography and History are making much use of visual aids and incorporate the intelligent discussion of current events. Drawing is very systematically treated, and although the results at present are not very advanced, there is every sign of steady progress and development.

Some special features were noted which deserve commendation: The older boys are encouraged to discuss their hobbies, interests, and personal experiences under conditions which give them an insight into the rules of orderly debate. School journeys for sketching, historical research, and geographical survey have been undertaken.

The teaching of Handicraft has not yet developed into a definite training in a graded procedure associated with other school subjects. One of the assistant Masters who has some ideas on the subject has it in his charge, and he has exercised the boys in the use of raffia and cane. They have done some good work on the lines laid down, which however, admit of little or no differentiation between the work of standard 4 and standard 6. These materials are not best suited to boys use, nor are they the best means of approach to the technical work of the Manual Room. The manual Instructor in charge of this room is systematic and thorough in his teaching, has a high standard of requirement, and gets good work from his boys. It lingers somewhat over the early stages of tool usage, and might with advantage to the more capable boys, be more advanced in the art of construction and in the use of initiative.

Provision should be made in this room for means of leading promising boys to the use of more difficult materials as their mental and physical powers develop.

Teaching Staff

- F B Potter, Head Teacher
- A Beales
- J H Kew
- H Abe
- C H Bristow
- W H M Crohan
- A H Withers
- N W Dingley.
- L Watson
- C H Allison Handicraft Instructor

H M Inspectors Report 1953

Inspected on 21-24th October 1953

Nature and scope of School

This had been a Senior School for some years before 1945 when it was given the status of a secondary school. Its catchments area stretches from the closely built streets that flank the docks, with their warehouses and storage yards, to include more spacious and fairly recently built housing estates. Most of the boys come from fair contributing primary schools, about 170 being admitted each year. At the age of 12 or 13 some 20 boys a year are transferred to other schools for secondary grammar or technical courses. The Great Education Authority's System of transfer is such that some pupils move from junior(paid) to secondary schools just before they are 11 years of age. Thus, during the autumn term the school contains some boys who are in their fifth year but must remain at school until the end of term before they are old enough to leave. Numbers are usually more than 700 at the beginning of the school year but this year they were 695 when the inspection took place. The Careers Master keeps detailed record of the work taken up by the boys when they leave the school. According to his classification, which appears to be reasonable, 253 of the 485 boys who left during the last three years took up work of a skilled or semi-skilled nature and 232 routine works. The proportion of leavers who enter the first category appears to have increased each year during the period under review.

Governing Body

There are ten Governors, three of them women. Six are members of the Borough Council and four co-opted. They act jointly for this and the adjoining Girls' School.

Premises and Equipment

The site of two and a half acres and the main building, which was completed little more than 20 years ago, are shared between this school and a girls' secondary school about the same size. Hutted classrooms were added under the H O R S A scheme. There are no proper playing fields and the two acres of land that constitute the school garden are part of public allotments and are 10 minutes walk from the school. The Boys' School possesses eighteen classrooms, two workshops and a very small hall. Provided the forms are large there are numerically enough teaching spaces for the present number of pupils. Unfortunately many of them are of the wrong sort for the various activities associated with secondary education today. The school lacks large rooms that could be equipped for teaching those subjects commonly referred to as "practical", not only are the Masters handicapped in their treatment of such subjects but also the curriculum itself is restricted. There is no immediate prospect of extensions to the site and additional accommodation could only be provided by making serious inroads upon the already insufficient playground space. It would, therefore, appear that major improvements must wait until a reduction in the number of pupils attending the school permits structural alterations.

Regular experimental work by the boys in Science is impossible since the subject is taught in Form rooms, which, in spite of satisfactorily improvised equipment, are not a good substitute for properly designed laboratories.

For Art the sloping dual desks are unsuitable and neither of the rooms used has a sink and draining board or good display boards. The hall affords but cramped space for Physical Education and the boys have to change in the corridor where there are no means of stacking or hanging clothing. In order that the floor of the hall may be kept clean, large mats are needed in the corridor approaching it. Two workshops are not enough for a school of this size! Many boys do not start woodwork until their third year. None of the rooms used for teaching Geography contains a good range of equipment for it. Lack of storage, a general source of inconvenience is particularly onerous to Masters responsible for teaching Technical Drawing and Crafts both of which employ a large amount of small equipment. There is no School Library but Form libraries have been vigorously built up and now contain about 1,600 books, nearly one third of them reference books and the remainder suitable fiction.

Much of the equipment is satisfactory and there are several examples of sensible adaptions by the Headmaster and Staff to overcome shortage of space. Some new sets of books are needed for English, Religious Instruction and Music. Some small improvements in the sanitary arrangements were suggested. In the garden a shed would provide storage for tools and shelter against sudden storms and a greenhouse would make it possible to attempt a more varied programme. The equipment in one of the workshops shows evidence of neglect and ill usage. Good use is made of the excellent electric gramophone, a filmstrip projector and a diascope. The school has also the part use of a cine-projector.

Staff

The Headmaster, who holds a degree of Master of Arts of the University of Sheffield, came to this school in 1948 after long experience as an Assistant in a Grammar School. He knows the school well and has given careful thought to its problems. He has evolved a clean-cut organisation suitable to the school's needs and has given it a sense of direction and purpose.

Of the 22 Assistant Masters, who comprise the full time staff, six hold posts of special responsibility. A part time Mistress who comes to the school each afternoon has the sole task of giving remedial teaching to retarded pupils. Half the Masters have joined the staff since 1947 and nearly all of them have had but short experience of teaching. With one exception the rest form a core of competent and experienced practitioners. The teaching strength of the staff as a whole is satisfactory. There are several Masters with ability above the average and there is only one very weak teacher. Several of the younger masters show considerable promise.

By training an interest the staff is able to deal adequately with most subjects. In Art and Craft, Music and Physical Education, however, a full range of work cannot be attempted because the Masters concerned have not had the appropriate specialist training. Many Masters give generously of their time in the development of out of school activities.

Organisation, Curriculum and Standard of Work

There are four Streams graded and called A, B, C, and D, making 16 forms. Two extra forms are made up as follows; the Headmaster divides the largest single age group into five instead of four forms. At present it is in the second year, which is so divided. The boys in their fifth year are in one form and this exists only during the autumn term. In the first two years the C and D forms are kept as small as possible.

The curriculum contains the usual subjects taught in secondary modern schools. The A forms pursue a four year course in French and the remaining forms do Gardening instead. All forms except 1C and 1D have Technical Drawing and time is given to the C and D forms throughout the school for general crafts. There is no music in the fourth year or for form 3A. Handicrafts are confined to third and fourth years and forms 2A and 2B. In the lower forms the time devoted to English is rather generous. The boys in forms 5, 4A, 4B and 4C give nearly the whole of one afternoon each week to what are termed projects. For this purpose they are divided into groups, which are related not to forms but to the boys interest; the topics that they deal with extend beyond the usual boundaries of subjects. Much of the work is carried out by small groups of individual boys and worthwhile results are achieved not only in what is produced but also in the valuable experience of working as members of a team.

Subjects are taught mainly on a specialised basis with usually two, three or four Masters to each subject. In some cases the work is divided according to streams and in other cases according to year groups. English, however, is taught by one form Master, and there are seven Masters involved in the teaching of Religious Instruction. Viewed as a whole, the curriculum and organisation have been sensibly designed to meet the needs of the boys and to make the best of limited facilities.

In one important aspect, however, arrangement for the D stream needs reconsideration. While most of the teaching for these slower pupils is successfully adapted to their capacities, basic instruction in English and Mathematics is entrusted in several forms to young Masters with neither the specialised training nor the experience for it. Good results are being achieved by the remedial Mistress but her contribution needs strengthening in the Form room. The conquest of illiteracy for as many boys as possible in forms 1D calls for the services of a skilful teacher.

Work of good quality is done in Religious Instruction, History and Technical Drawing. Nearly all the subjects reach a satisfactory level, some of them being above average and others unevenly developed. In one workshop the standards achieved in Handicrafts are very low. The neatness with which written work is set out and the legibility of the handwriting are commendable features.

Subjects of Instruction

Religious Instruction

The Headmaster and six Masters share the teaching of Religious Instruction and all forms devote two periods weekly to it. The teaching based on the Agreed Syllabus, is sincere and the lessons generally well prepared. The Headmaster has made good use of the individual talents of his staff and the pupils respond well. In all forms simple records are kept; informal individual recording might advantageously be introduced in certain forms. An abridged addition of the bible is used in all forms and the more capable pupils might now have the opportunity to familiarise themselves with the full bible. The obvious sincerity with which the subject is treated provides a strong beneficial influence throughout the school.

English

In each form the English teaching is undertaken by the Form Master. The A and B streams follow a similar scheme while there are separate schemes for C and S streams. The time allowed varies from 10 weekly lessons in the first year to six in the fourth year.

Spoken English is given considerable attention and various kinds of oral work are supplemented by separate lessons for Drama in the first two years and in forms 3B and 5. A well-informed drama scheme has been drawn up and what was heard suggested that the lessons are contributing usefully to confidence and fluency in speaking. Some of the work culminates in the acting of plays, in which the school appears to be providing a valuable experience and establishing its own traditions. Written work is regular and with few exceptions exercise books are neat and handwriting legible. In the A and B forms progress towards correctly written English is satisfactory; errors of spelling are perhaps less common in the fourth year than failings in expression and syntax, to which the correction might give rather more attention. The abler and older boys produce some well written accounts in their "Projects" and compositions are painstaking. In some forms personal writing books, not subject to formal correction, reveal some lively stories and accounts. The C and D Forms present a particular problem of backwardness, which is being tackled with determination in co-operation with the Child Guidance Service. Small groups of backward readers receive remedial tuition from a visiting teacher and a number of boys show measurable improvement, but this work needs the backing of more experienced teaching in one or two of the D Forms. In general the lessons devoted to literature are not as fruitful as they might be. The school is in the process of improving the range and quantity of books for class work and this should allow an enrichment of this part of the work. Form libraries are much used and are encouraging many boys to read who would not otherwise do so.

In so large a school with so wide a range of ability in the many forms, each taught by a different member of the staff, no general assessment will suffice, but the impression remains that seriousness of purpose

pervades the work in the classroom and that, though much remains to be done, standards of English seem to be rising.

History

Each of the 3 Masters who teach History makes a good contribution to its development in the school. The scheme is in the main, concerned with British History.

During the first three years the course extends from Roman times to early nineteenth century. In the fourth year the story is brought up to our own times largely through the medium of topics which deal with various aspects of social history and in this part of the scheme there is a danger that History may be divorced from the great personalities who shaped it.

All the Masters have been concerned to preserve a balance between maintaining the chronological flow and making occasional detailed studies of particular periods. The resultant blend is successful. Pictures and filmstrips are used to advantage. The boys learn to read carefully and to record what they have discovered and their knowledge of History is very creditable.

Geography

One form is taken by its Form Master but the rest of the teaching is shared by three Masters. Continual studies form the basis of the work and visual aids play an important part in the presentation. No attempt is made to cover the whole world but what is done is treated thoroughly and suitable aspects of physical geography are stressed. Some of the earlier work is approached much more formally than the scheme suggests and training in the reading of maps is not progressively linked with the main themes. Apart from these criticisms the course has been satisfactorily varied according to the different abilities of the boys. Lessons are interesting and well prepared and many forms are receiving good training in observation, reading and original writing. Some outdoor work is done during school journeys and locally and this is being extended through the study of a farm. The boys reveal a good knowledge of the work done and an understanding of many geographical relationships.

French

The A Forms are taught by two members of the staff. The senior master has made many visits abroad, sometimes with parties of boys from the school; he teaches with enthusiasm and a firm belief in the values of the subject. The other master has only this term succeeded another member of the staff in teaching forms 1A and 3A, he has made steady progress with the first year pupils, who show keenness and have already gained a useful vocabulary and a good idea of pronunciation. In the later forms there is some good work, but progress is slower, and achievement is disappointing in form 4A. This may be largely the result of some conflict of method in the teaching of the previous year. The lessons rightly lay emphasis on oral work, but they require more variation; rapid reading of simple French texts and the building of compositions from short sentences on a connected theme are well within the capabilities of the boys and might be used more frequently to consolidate knowledge.

Four weekly lessons are given except to Form 4A, which have three. With the present staff and with some extension and alignment of methods there appears to be no reason why the scheme should not be successful and fulfil the promise, which it now shows.

Mathematics

Three Masters take the A, B, and C forms respectively and another three cover the work in the D forms. This is a satisfactory arrangement and most of the teaching shows an appreciation of the needs of the boys . The syllabus is suitably adjusted and the A and B forms have, in addition to Arithmetic, Algebra, Logarithms and more graphical work. Arithmetical applications might be introduced earlier, and less able boys might be given graphical work, and the ablest simple trigonometry. The standard of presentation is good and written exercises generally based on groups are done accurately. Although practice is given in mental exercises this important side of the work as seen during the inspection is neither sufficiently stimulating nor demanding.

The A forms react favourably to their more demanding course; the B forms are not yet working to capacity, owing to the Masters' inexperience, but there is steady progress in both the B and C forms, the work in the D forms is not always satisfactory.

Science

All the boys have a course in General Science and those in the first forms have nature study in addition. Two Masters share the teaching of the main course; one is an experienced teacher, with a practical knowledge of Science and the other is just beginning his teaching career. Their work is severely handicapped by very poor facilities. Practical work by the boys is virtually impossible until the fifth year and in the project group where numbers are small, of necessity demonstrations with explanations or discussions are as successful as circumstances permit. The boys are reasonably interested and gain some understanding of their environment, and forms 4A and B are using simple reference books to help in note taking. This practice might well be started earlier if suitable books can be provided. The Master responsible for nature study is inexperienced with this work, which is, at present, treated too academically and without sufficient variation for the different forms.

Gardening

The four Masters who teach this subject have conscientiously devoted their efforts to the clearance of the site and the development of the garden under difficult conditions. The soil is poor, yet useful crops have been grown and in addition a small lawn, rockeries and flower gardens have been laid out. Much has been achieved and still more is contemplated; the Masters are determined to overcome the difficulties and the boys work with enthusiasm. Now that worthwhile results have been achieved in routine cropping more experimental work might with advantage be included and the propagation of fruit, flowering shrubs and roses might be introduced. Suitable explanatory labels could be maintained so that all forms might benefit from the experiments. With the full co-operation of the Masters in charge of Handicrafts, the construction, by the boys, of cold frames, a garden shelter, storage facilities and a greenhouse should not prove insuperable.

Handicrafts

Owing to the shortage of woodworking rooms, only the 10 upper forms can benefit from this training, but the other forms receive some compensatory craftwork in lieu of woodwork. One workshop of adequate dimensions is situated on the first floor and the other, of temporary construction, lies across the playground. The general range of equipment in each workshop is satisfactory and in both rooms suitable woodworking lathes have recently been installed.

Two qualified experienced Masters share the teaching: each form is divided equally and the two halves are taught simultaneously in the two workshops. The workshop within the main building is well organised, the equipment is well maintained and the Master has devoted considerable thought to the planning of his work. The general standard of craftsmanship achieved is satisfactory. As the course is only two, or, at the most, three years long, the range of work attempted tends to be rather restricted.

Aware of this difficulty the Master is seeking to increase the possible range, and with a reduction on the time spent on drawing – (somewhat unnecessary having regard to the good work done in Technical Drawing) – and the introduction of duplicated drawings, an earlier approach to constructive work might be secured. The boys, however, do show considerable skill in the manipulation of tools

and derive benefit from their training. The future possibility of group work in building cold frames, a garden shed and a greenhouse was discussed at the time of the inspection.

The other workshop does not produce comparable work. The Master fails to maintain the equipment provided; pupils are allowed to chisel on the bare bench tops, several vices are insecurely mounted, many vice cheeks are badly worn and one or two are completely missing. Bench tops are badly worn, some are missing and many need replacement. Most planes need re-mounting and the edge tools are not sharp; no tool racks are suitable and tools which do not fit the bench cupboard are allowed to hang from the window stays. The cumulative effect of neglected maintenance and ineffective organisation is reflected in the low standard of work seen, some faulty techniques are allowed to persist and the pupils, although anxious to succeed, fail to do so.

Technical Drawing

Except for 1C and 1D, all boys devote at least two periods weekly to Technical Drawing. Two Masters are responsible for this teaching; the four-year course is soundly conceived and well taught. During the first year pupils spend most of their time on geometric drawing. Later the course expands to cover an interesting range of work, which provides a sound introduction to the theory of drawing. Good standards of draughtsmanship are maintained; the pupils clearly reflect the enthusiasm of the Masters and the subject develops well. The increased use of actual solid objects might add further zest and clarity to the work while the occasional use of squared and isometric paper might save time spent on actual drawing technique, and so increase the possible amount of theory. Having regard to the enthusiasm and considerable achievement within the work, some more accurate drawing instruments might be supplied when conditions permit. The making of blue prints could add further interest and some simple surveying could widen the field of work attempted by the older pupils.

Art and Craft

Art and Crafts are taught in ordinary classrooms without adequate facilities. Art lessons are given by two Masters while other Masters take additional Craft lessons with C and D forms. There are separate courses for Art and Craft. The work done in the Art lessons is limited to certain aspects of drawing and painting with some lettering. The craft lessons are concerned mainly with technical exercises in simple bookbinding. There is room for broadening the range of work especially in the Art lessons and a reconsideration of aims might well suggest a closer co-ordination between Arts and Crafts. Much of the work done in the Art lesson does not give enough opportunity for developing the creative powers of the majority of the boys; a few individuals have produced promising work particularly as a result of observation, but there is a general need for a more confident approach and for more flexible use of media. Sound work is being done in book crafts where the boys have a useful training in precision. Some interesting experiments in three-dimensional designs have been attempted and might be extended. The Masters concerned with Art and Crafts are capable teachers of general subjects who maintain the boys' interests by thorough instruction, but this large school lacks the help, which could be given by a well-qualified specialist in the subject.

Music

It is regrettable that Music is so poorly developed in a school of this size. It is not the fault of the young Master who has been given the task of teaching it, for though he is interested in music he has not had the necessary training to do justice to it. This is particularly evident in the singing, which is marred not only by poor diction, uncertain pitch and rough tone but also by the absence of a progressively arranged scheme of songs. More success is achieved in teaching the beginnings of musical appreciation.

The boys are being introduced to some good recorded music and are learning something about the great composers.

Physical Education

Five Masters share the teaching of gymnastics and games and although they are without special qualifications in Physical Education they take the lessons in a careful and conscientious manner. The boys are kept well occupied along somewhat stereotyped lines and the standard of work reaches a satisfactory but not high standard. Class control and general lesson arrangements are good but the performance of movements in the main and in unison is sometimes over emphasised, individual work might be better represented and more expected of the pupils mentally. The lack of a proper playing field has not hampered unduly the development of the games side although in cricket and athletic field events, some restriction is evident. However, the school takes a full part in level sporting competitions and the teams and its representatives have enjoyed many successes. An athletic meeting, a cross – country race and swimming gala are held annually, throughout the year, parties visit the local baths for swimming instruction and the majority of the boys learn to swim. In addition, the value of walking and camping holidays has not been overlooked and groups have enjoyed these pursuits in the Lake District and at Stratford upon Avon.

General Activities and Corporate Life

For daily assembly the upper and lower forms meet on alternative mornings because the hall is not large enough for the whole school to come together. Boys read the lessons and the service is simple and appropriate. About 150 boys and Masters are provided with school dinners daily and they have to walk to a meals centre where the surroundings have been made as bright as possible. The meal observed was good and adequate in quantity and waste was negligible. The present dinner scheme runs smoothly and the boys conduct themselves well but it might eventually be possible to offer greater opportunities for social training by introducing a table service.

The interest taken by members of the staff in out of school activities has already been attended to in this report. In addition to games and sport, which play an important part in the life of the boys, Hobbies, Drama, and a Field Club find a place in the programme and visits are made to distant parts of the country and occasionally abroad. Through the efforts of the Careers Master, boys in their last term are kept well informed about the kind of jobs that are available and conditions of work.

A system of prefects has been instituted and though their duties are not, as yet, extensive the value of building up a

responsible attitude on the part of these boys is recognised. The large majority of the boys have responded well to the encouragement that has been given to good personal grooming. Throughout the Inspection their behaviour was good.

General Conclusions

In spite of the poor facilities that the school possesses for its present numbers positive achievements are being made. The boys are clearly progressing intellectually and socially. The aesthetic side still needs to be developed.

Above: an early example of a boys school report
Opposite: A later 1960s example report

ATTENDANCE .... *Satisfactory* .... CONDUCT .... *V. Good.*

ATTAINMENTS AND APTITUDES :-

Of average ability in the "3" Form.
He has done well in his practical
work particularly in woodwork.

R. A. Marwell.
(Asst. Head of Carer.)

HEADMASTER'S REPORT *A boy of remarkably good*
ability who has worked well. He
is of excellent character. He has
a pleasant disposition, and
should be a capable and
dependable employee.

Headmaster *A.P.Lee*

Date *July 1960.*

RESULT OF LAST FORM EXAMINATION

		Form Pos.	Master's Initial
ENGLISH	*Fair*	19/30	*EG*
MATHS	*Fair.*	14th/29 3rd	*EG*
TECHNICAL DRAWING	*Satisfactory*	13/30	*JH*
SCIENCE	*Good*	12/30	*JH*
BIOLOGY	*Good*	8/30	*JH*
NATURE STUDY			
WOODWORK	*Very Good (1st in exam)*	1/10	
METALWORK	*He has done good work*	9/15	*E.G*
FRENCH			
HISTORY	*Satisfactory.*	19/30	*WDd*
GEOGRAPHY	*Satisfactory.*	14/29	*WDd*
RELIGIOUS INSTRUCTION	*Good*		*G.*
HANDICRAFT			
GARDENING			
PHYSICAL EDUCATION	*Fair*	—	*EG*

7: EDUCATIONAL OUTINGS

Many trips were arranged for the boys with a variety of locations covering a wide spectrum of subjects and activities during the reign of the school. This chapter illustrates some of these through the photos and writings of pupils.

Trip to the Sacré Cœur with Mr Withers

As well as sporting activities for football, athletics, cricket, swimming, cross country running and boxing, the arts also played a major role with drama, music, choirs and, even, ballet. Ballroom dancing was later taught at school. There were visits to the local factories and docks in the area for career purposes for the older pupils about to leave school. The majority of trips consisted of small parties of approximately 24 boys accompanied by teachers on a day's event. However during the summer months a full week's vacation was planned on a regular basis from 1946 to certain locations where the boys camped and cooked for themselves as well as participating in outdoor activities and visits to places of interest and factories.

Some of these popular places were: Stratford upon Avon, Portsmouth Dockyard, Humberstone YMCA camp and Paris.

School Camp 1955

The boys were expected to look after themselves and write about their experiences and the places of interest they saw when on outings. A fine example of this is one book **"School Camp 1955"** which Mr Nowell had kept in his possession. His family has kindly allowed us to publish it. The pages illustrate the neat hand writing, use of English language and content.

School Camp 1955 - The Party

Stratford-upon-Avon.
The Journey from Grimsby to Stratford.

Twenty four boys excited and over anxious scrambled eagerly on a Stark's bus. With rucksacks and the school's folding canoe on the rear seat of the bus, the tents and kitbags were stacked in the "boot" of the bus.

With everything ready we departed waving good-bye to a few mournful mothers but I am sure at the back of their minds glad to see the last of us for a week. We were on our way at 9.45 on Monday the 13th June.

The journey was a long one but I was not in the least uninterested because my companions and I were kept in trim by numerous groans representing modern songs. Now I know why England's countryside is so famous. Haymaking was popularity in most fields along with a feverish perfumed smell. The birds uttered a few rapturous and waiting patiently for an answer. Mother Nature had not failed us again this year for the countryside was brightened up by her wonderous work.

The first place of interest was Lincoln City. I was astonished at the towering cathedral with its skilful sculpturing some of the best in England. The towers fascinated me the most, standing vertically making the houses below look like dwarfs.

With Lincoln City in the distance slowly fading away we made our way towards Newark. Newark came into sight while passing along several narrow roads I noticed some very old houses obviously awaiting demolition.

At Newark a 30 minutes break was summoned by one of our two masters. My colleagues and I had

a short snack and made our way towards the waiting bus. All this time our driver had kept us skilfully on the A46 route to Stratford.

Leaving Newark far behind and feeling better for my snack, I was continually observing England's countryside. The sun had decided to break through the overcast clouds making the interior of the bus rather stifling but the windows were opened and the fresh air was gladly welcomed. Leicester loomed in the distance. While travelling on a surprisingly excellent road I noticed a special path for pedal cyclists to ride on. On top of a shoe-making factory stood the small form of the Statue of Liberty.

Leaving Leicester we found ourselves entering Coventry made famous by Lady Godiva. Coventry has a great industrial importance due to their car producing factories. Coventry survived the first of the German bomber attacks during the war. A coal-mine stood on the outskirts of Coventry spurting smoke like black clouds of death. Although going alongside many railway lines and stations a train could not be found in motion.

Warwick was our next place of ancient history. Passing through the town centre we saw Warwick Castle surrounded by beautiful gardens. Its walls have stopped many enemy armies wishing to overpower the castle.

A journey not too long brought us happily into Stratford in which was the camp-site. A few roofs of caravans leapt by as we were now turning in a gateway to the camp-site.

With everything unloaded our "homes" were

soon erected and our first meal on the Pri-Mus was well on the way to completion.

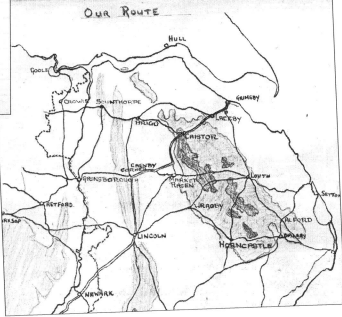

OUR ROUTE

The Camp Site

As we drew into the camp site the first thing that caught our eyes was the River Avon glittering in the bright sunshine. We were welcomed by a lady and gentleman named Mr. and Mrs. Cosgrove and also their daughter, Shirley. As we descended from the bus our first job was to clear the grass for erecting our tents which were given out by Mr. Nowell and Mr. Hollingworth.

Then we started to measure the correct distances between each tent and after being given advice we erected our tents in one straight line. When our tents were up we were then given the primus stoves, windscreens and water buckets and last of all our bed-roll in which we had to sleep for six days.

By the banks of the river were many willow trees and on the opposite side a small hut. Next to the camp-site was a caravan site from where we drew our water.

At the side of the camp was the A46 road where many transport lorries were carrying fish from Grimsby and Hull, coal, timber and tractors named Fergusons on their way to a tractor show. A hundred yards from the camp-site is the open air bathing pool. To the north is Warwick reached by two routes the A46 and the A429. and in the south is Stratford which is about a mile from the camp-site.

On the east side is the grassy hills over which we walked. As we reached the top we looked down we saw Stratford-upon-Avon surrounded by meadows separated by trees of many different species such as the elm, the sycamore,

the lime and the beech. There were thrushes and blackbirds whistling in the tree tops while the swans were gliding peacefully on the River Avon.

by A. Smith

COOKING IN CAMP

Twenty four boys were privileged to have a week out of school under canvas so they could visit Stratford upon Avon.

There were two boys to a tent and we all had to cook our own food by means of primus stoves.

Our tent was a ridge tent which when completed had a fly sheet. The purpose of having a fly sheet is so that it will keep the tent perfectly dry in wet weather, cool in hot weather and warm in cold weather.

On the ground under the fly sheet we stored our canteen, washbowl bucket, primus and windscreen. In the bucket we had to keep the milk so as to keep it fresh in hot weather. At night we had to slacken off the guy ropes and tighten them again in the morning because the dew or rain makes the ropes shrink.

During the week we learnt how to pitch a tent properly, how to cook properly with a primus stove, how to find and organise a proper camp site, to pitch a tent and how to put up a windscreen to prevent any wind blowing the primus flame out.

Before we pitched camp the first difficulty we found was that the ground was waterlogged so we had to pitch camp on the higher ground but before this the long-grass had to be cut and made firm to make it comfortable for us to-lie on.

Then we marked out the positions for each tent. When this was finished we commenced to put down the ground sheet and then tested the ground for comfort.

The tents were all put up in a big curve the teachers tent being the first. Next to it was a small tent where we kept the spare equipment.

By the end of the week we had learn a lot and felt capable of going camping ourselves.

Stratford-upon-Avon

Stratford-upon-Avon is the most famous of England's market towns by reason of its great townsman, William Shakespeare who was born in 1564 and died in 1616. It is situated in the heart of England with the beauty of its riverside settings as it was in the period of Shakespeare. The industries of the present day are light such as beer brewing, fruit canning, the making of road signs and aluminium goods.

The lay-out of the streets and names have changed little since the fourteenth. The stone Clopton Bridge which carries most of the traffic over the Avon was built nearly five centuries ago.

The River Avon glides gracefully along through Stratford with the Memorial Theatre and Holy Trinity church standing majestically among the cottages with their straw roofs and chimney stacks clustered on a gentle slope. The architecture of the town is of the fifthteenth century, the type of Shakespeare's time. Shakespeare's Birthplace and other buildings associated with him are preserved as a memorial to Shakespeare where people from all towns and countries come for sight seeing.

Three main roads run into Stratford the Warwick Road runs 8 miles from Warwick to join the Broadway Rd. The road branches into four, to the right is High St which leads to the Grammar school and Holy Trinity College. Forking off High St is Wood St which leads to the hospital, the station and also to Shottery.

Shakespeare's Birthplace is situated in Henley St and New Place in High St. The Memorial Theatre is situated by the side of the River Avon and further down the River Avon is Holy Trinity Church.

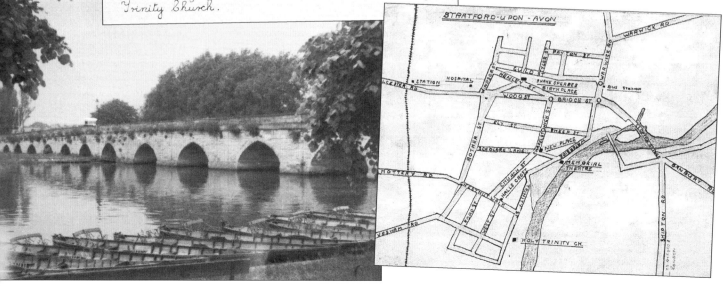

Shakespeare's Birthplace.

William Shakespeare, the famous poet, author and playwright was born in Stratford-upon-avon in the year 1564 and unfortunately died in 1616 making him only 52.

We smartly walked down Henley Street towards Shakespeare's Birthplace on Tuesday 14th June 1955. After greeting members of the Shakespeare Trust we assembled ourselves and started to view the first room.

The first room namely the parlour, had an Elizabethan fireplace, not the original, made of oak beams. The pots were hung on large chains plugged into the wall. Cooking utensils were made of bronze arranged around the open fireplace.

The second room now a museum was once the workshop of Shakespeare's father John Shakespeare. Here are numerous glass cases displaying documents on which is written Shakespeare's actual signature. Coins used in those days are also on display. A most valuable exhibit is the First Folio of Shakespeare's plays.

Another museum the third room on the first floor is wide and gracious with only little lighting which was made only by glass and rush. In a glass in this museum is a document saying that Shakespeare inherited most of his property which was later bequeathed by Lady Elizabeth. Also in this room is a bust of Shakespeare and an ancient oak desk.

The Birth Room, the room in which Shakespeare was born is upstairs. On the leaded windows names of famous men of the day were scratched such as Isaac Watts, Sir Walter Scott

and Thomas Carlisle. The bed in the room is not a "four poster" they were only for the richer people. At the bottom of the bed is a bible box in which was kept the family treasure, the bible. A wooden cradle is situated in one corner of the room but is not the original.

Leading from the Birth Room is a small bedroom with a wide bed probably Shakespeare himself slept in this bed sometime during his life.

Coming downstairs again we walk through an archway into a kitchen which has the familiar bronze plates and an open fireplace with a spit. Among other utensils is a chopping board 250 years old. The actual door of the shop is in this kitchen brought in for preservation. In this room is a wooden baby-minder. There is a wine cellar which is unsafe.

Now at the end of our visit we entered a most beautiful garden. On a blossomed apple can be found mistletoe.

Warwick Castle.

At approximately 7.30 A.M. on Friday, 4th June, we arose to prepare our breakfast. Everybody was excited because it was the day we were to visit Warwick castle.

Ready for the journey we commenced to walk to the bus station, where we ascended a corporation bus to take the A429 route to Warwick.

Beautiful scenery decorated the country side and it was clear that Mother Nature had been busily working, making her task a glorious sight.

We finally reached our destination and alighting from the bus at Warwick market place we made our way to the castle.

On entering, I noticed the huge, ugly looking port cullis which was directly above the gateway, and walking further on I saw the keep, known as Ethelfleda's Mound.

The castle itself looked a wonderful sight with its magnificent battlements and towers. A flag pole stood proudly on one of the towers and the absence of the flag told us that the Earl of Warwick was not in residence. The castle grounds are very beautiful are well looked after, but the grandeur of this castle is enhanced by its river setting.

We met our guide who first of all took us into the armoury where many exhibits including crossbows, swords, musket, horse-pistols, and other relics were on show. Most of the armour was Cromwellian and it is cleaned once a week by an attendant.

After passing many distinguished paintings we entered the Earl of Warwick's private chapel. It was a small room with a

beautiful altar and wooden pews. The windows were stained glass and many famous paintings of the 14th. century were hung on the wall. also Chinese cane chairs were arranged in suitable positions. Coming out of the Chapel we passed along a corridor, and there we saw more paintings. Then we entered an exquisite dining room in which was elaborate furniture. A huge glass chandelier hung from the ceiling, and also at one end of the room was a magnificent painting of Charles I by Van Dyck.

When we were fully informed of the Dining Room we crossed a hall and entered into a 14th century banquet hall. The floor is made of flagstone. Armour decorates the room, one of the pieces is an armoured horse and rider. Another is a 16th century German warriors which is quite heavy. Also is a puritan hat not made of leather but iron. A double handed ceremonial sword hangs up on one of the 10 ft. thick walls Antelopes horns which hang high up in the banquet hall are the oldest exhibits in the castle, because they are 2,000 years old. I seeing the window is a large, ugly looking cannon which was used on a French man o' war ship.

The Drawing Room was the next we visited and it looked very inviting. Tapestry hung round the walls and big glass cabinets were in suitable places.

Text was the cedar room where all panels and doors were made of cedar wood. The carpet, which was French, was 140 yrs.

old. A marble topped table, which was very old, dates back to the 18 century. Paintings by Van Dyck, and Sir Josiah Reynolds hung all round the room.

Then we entered the old music room where more paintings were to be seen one being a Spanish warrior. In one corner was a very valuable table from Venice with an inlaid marble top.

Then the guide led us into Queen Anne's bed chamber where stood a splendid four postered bed. Hanging on one of the walls was tapestry and it was 351 years old. It was the cleverly patterned ceiling that made the room look distinguished.

We then entered the Lady's room where a black marble table inlaid with flowers stood in a corner. All the walls were carved contrasting with the patterned ceiling

The guide then pressed a secret spring and a panel swung open to admit us to the haunted room where a painting of Fulke Greville by Patoun hung.

Our tour rou'd the interior of the castle ended, we went into the castle grounds and passing the moat which was hand dug we entered into the paradise of the Italian gardens where peacocks were roaming about. We walked down an avenue of trees to an ornamental fish-pond where beautiful fish were basking in the sun. On a large summer house we saw the Warwick Vase which is two thousand three hundred years old. Satisfied with the visit to Warwick we walked back to the Market Place where we boarded a bus for Stratford.

Shottery

William Shakespeare married Anne Hathaway who lived in a cottage at Shottery which lies to the south Stratford.

On Thursday we were to visit Shottery and as the day was fine and hot we decided to go by the country to Shottery using our ordinance maps as a guide. We set off in groups of six and had to find our own way without the teachers. Our route lay across Clopton Bridge through the Cricket Ground along the left bank of the river. We passed the Memorial Theatre, Holy Trinity Church and a Weir and Keeping to the river bank we came to a railway embankment shown on our maps. Here we crossed the river by a bridge, passed under the railway and continued through many fields following the right bank of the river until we came to a railway over a viaduct. From our maps we had to pass under the railway and turn right following a race course. Then we came to a road which was sign-posted to Shottery which we reached after an interesting and very pleasant journey of about an hour.

Anne Hathaway's cottage was an old fashioned, thatched roof cottage with a lovely garden of old time flowers. Our guide took us round to see many interesting things. In the first room there was a very large open fire place, some old fashioned oak chests and some old chairs of Anne Hathaway's time In the second room we went in there was an old spinning wheel in the corner with which the raw wool was spun into yarn. There was another fire place and more old fashioned chairs of Anne Hathaway's time. After this we went up stairs and the first room was the bedroom of Anne Hathaway. This contained a bedstead fitted with rush matting. The bed bed its self was made of four oak pillows and at the floor

of the bed was fitted a bible box used for putting the bible and jewellery in. At the foot of the bed was a small wooden cot. As we went into the next room it was nearly the same as the first one except there was no bed but still another rush mat on the floor other wise it would have been the naked wooden floor. After this we came down into the kitchen where there was a large polished top table that was used for eating off and could be reversed for working on and for getting the dinner ready. In the kitchen was a large fire place, a dole box for alms, a large oak cupboard and also a large drinking vessel called a Black Jack. This needed a strong arm for lifting when full. Out side the cottage there was a lovely orchard where we took some photographs and after this we journeyed back to camp

Bournville.

At about half past eight our party of campers set off for Bournville in a Stratford Blue Bus, a trip which we had looked forward to very much, after an hour's journey through the Warwickshire countryside we arrived at Bournville.

Our first port of call was a large hall where we were shown a film called "Cocao Harvest." This Documentary explained to us how the cocoa pods were grown the beans extracted, dried, packed and shipped to Bournville.

From there we were split up into small groups and escorted by guides round the machines. We were shown the beans ground down into fine powder and mixed, in large vats, to make the liquid chocolate.

After that we went round to a machine which made the tins and on to others which cut the cardboard and made the boxes for the various products. There were girls standing by who stuck

on pictures and ribbon.

After that we went round to a machine which made the boxes for their exports which were stretched over a very large area.

Then after going round mechanical devices which automaticaly wrapped and packed the chocolates, the guide took us into a canteen where we were offered the choice of cocoa chocolate or ovaltine with some biscuits.

Later we resumed our tour of the factory. All around us there were conveyer belts carrying assorted centres and biscuits which passed under a grill pouring chocolate over them. Sitting beside the conveyer belts women were putting appropriate designs on the assortments. These were wrapped and placed in boxes.

We were taken round numerous other departments too many in fact to mention every detail but finally we were presented, at the end of our tour of inspection, with a booklet and a box of samples.

Top to bottom:
Mr Hollingsworth
taking an early shave
Camp site
Canoeing
Mr Lee serving camp meals

Top to bottom:
Sketching by the riverside
Arrival at campsite
Waiting for departure to camp
Teaching the art of angling

8: TEACHING STAFF

This Chapter, describing the memoirs recorded by individual teachers, gives an insight into the daily routines and experiences of life as a teacher at Armstrong St School

Dennis Holah

M J D Holah was educated at Brigg Grammar School and after service in the R A F, went on to the City of Leeds Training College to become a teacher. His main discipline was Maths and Science and in June 1952 he was appointed as teacher at Armstrong Street Boys' School, where he undertook to teach various subjects including Gardening until the closure in July 1964.

At the time he was courting his future wife, Barbara Loveday who also lived in the same village of Keelby. They used to cycle to school from Keelby and, after they were wed, moved to their present address in Healing continuing to cycle to and from school. Mrs Holah was a Domestic Science Teacher in another Grimsby school.

After school, two nights a week, along with other members of staff, he would eat his sandwiches and work through to join Mr Marlborough's woodwork class from 7.00 to 9.00pm. When Mr Marlborough became Warden of all the Evening Institute classes at Armstrong, Mr Holah took over the woodwork classes, where he met many local characters from the West Marsh, i.e. Goody Taylor, sweet shop proprietor, Danny Bunn, the barber, etc.

Mr Holah was active in sports, playing football and cricket for local teams. He was an active member of the local Football Referees' Association and was often seen refereeing local games. He recalls the erection of cricket nets in the Watkin Street Hall and taking a course for the M C C Youth Coaching Certificate. Frank Tyson, the England fast bowler, came to present

the awards. His other hobbies included woodwork, camping, caravanning and travel.

He recalls that the Stevenson Dancing School used to visit to teach the boys giving dancing lessons in preparation for the annual Christmas dance held at the Winter Gardens with the Girls' School.

Mr Holah took part in a number of school excursions. Along with Mr Hotchkin they took a group to the Royal Naval Dockyard at Chatham for a week, the boys experiencing living in barracks. Another visit was a week at the Y M C A camp in SouthSea Lane at Humberstone.

There was a well-established camping club at school and, along with Mr Hotchkin, they would travel to the Y M C A camp at Fairthorne Manor, Botley, near Southampton for a week under canvas. Using a coach from Starks of Tetney (the driver camped on the back seat) visits were made to the Naval Dockyard at Portsmouth, including H M S Victory, Southampton Docks with an official guide, and a tour of the New Forest. A ferry ride to the Isle of Wight was also included to see the arrival/departure of one of the larger liners. The Union Castle line sailed for South Africa every Thursday at 4.00pm.

The teachers at the school were also capable of pranks on their own colleagues. Mr Holah recalls Mr Alf Lee had his car packed ready to drive to Cornwall on holiday and one member placed a fish on the engine and then shut the bonnet. They never found out how far he drove before the stench became unbearable! On another occasion a crab was nailed to the underside of his desk.

One day Mr Holah was passing a classroom and noticed a rabble of boys surrounding a blackboard with a large map of Asia pinned to it. Thinking they had been left unattended, he went in to restore order, only to find Mr Lee seated at the back of the room. "It's OK," he said, "There is a silver three penny piece on the table for the first boy to find Carlisle".

One year, when the leaving age was raised, Mr Holah was taken off normal timetable one afternoon a week to build a sailing dinghy with some of the boys who would normally have left. He was under pressure from M Lee who wanted to "try it out" during the summer holiday and the staff who, in jest, were trying to ensure the deadline was missed. The boat was named "The Shrimp" and Mr Lee organised sailing lessons for the boys in the dock. Mr Holah never did get a chance to sail in it.

The teachers used to use boys to send messages to each other asking to borrow a sweeping brush and the boy would come back with a paint brush.

A popular one was ''Mr (teacher's surname) sent me for the key to the Quadrangle''.

Mr Holah continued as a teacher in the Grimsby area until his retirement but stated that the time spent at Armstrong Street School and the colleagues he worked with there were some of the best moments of his teaching career and he often meets old pupils who remember the school and staff with affection.

Tom Herbert

Mr Herbert was in charge of gardening, a lesson very popular with the lads. The gardens, adjacent to the allotments off Corporation Road, covered an area larger than a football pitch and produced abundant crops the year round. Greens, potatoes, peas, beans, and bush fruits could be purchased by the boys for a few pence. The primary aim of the lessons was to develop a love of the soil. It was such hard work digging, forking, hoeing, raking, planting, weeding and harvesting

that I've often wondered since, if the boys immediate reaction, when facing a garden of their own, would be to hide the spade!

On three afternoons a week he would walk at the head of 40 boys, each carrying garden implements. He looked, he recalled, for all the world like Watt Tyler leading the Peasants' Revolt! One day I noticed out of the corner of my eye two boys, Walter Swinglehurst and Keith Waller, lagging behind as we passed allotments with rows of tempting peas. "They're not ready yet, Walter," I called out, "A good gardener should know they need rain to plump them out". The two looked guilty and it was a proud moment in my teaching career when I heard them whisper "You can't pull one over on Sir, he's real crafty".

Mr Herbert recalls the Open Day when he had the idea of displaying some of the boys' garden produce, the centre piece of which was to be a large bowl of blackcurrants.

Jimmy Spooner (I should have known better) was left in charge and at playtime I looked in to see how things were going and was aghast to see that there was little left of the luscious contents of the bowl. "The parents must have been sampling them," explained Jimmy. On seeing my look of disbelief, he added with an air of injured innocence, "You don't think I've eaten them, do you sir? How could I think such a thing?" I assured him, adding "All the same, it might not be a bad idea to wash those purple stains from your mouth before the head comes in! He might get suspicious".

Charles Merry (1942-46)

Mr Merry recalls walking the boys from school to Orwell St. Baths for swimming and then walking them back. The route meant walking along Corporation Road over the Bridge to Victoria St and up to Orwell St. He recalls one day on their return trip the bridge was up for boats bringing wood to Alexander Dock and had to wait half an hour before resuming the trip back to school. On his return the Headmaster, Mr Horn bellowed at him asking why he was late and, when told, replied that he should get there before the bridge went up! He recalls incendiary bombs fell into the Girls' small Hall but the watchers quickly put them out before any damage was done. During the war Armstrong School had to take on additional classes from South Parade and Macaulay St. Schools due to bomb damage and due to shortage of staff, women teachers were introduced to meet the education demand.

Mr Graham Holley

Mr Holley started at Armstrong School in July 1952 as a Sports Teacher and also taught Maths, Drama and undertook teaching Technical Drawing at evening classes.

He recalls being given a cane and shown the techniques of administrating it. He was known as "the young bugger" by his colleagues. The class sizes were 40+.

He recalls the war records of some of the serving teachers as follows:

Mr Alf Lee A major in the Homeguard

Mr Harry Abe involved in the D day landings

Mr Reg Dixon A paratrooper who had an accident during the war

Mr Alec Withers gassed in WW1

Mr Don Hotchkin despatch rider in N Africa

Mr R Fox Infantry Officer in N Africa wounded with fingers shot off on one hand

His main subject was as a P T Teacher and he taught the lads to play Basketball, Cricket, Football, and Athletics. Each year when the House matches were being played, the boys would walk to the venue, approximately 100 pupils, whilst he biked alongside the column of boys. When the football teams played at Immingham they would travel by tram. He recalls that the Chapman St. Buildings were used for school dinners, that he pursued alterations to allow indoor net practise for cricket and the installation of showers

in the early 1960s. He remembers taking a party of 20 boys with Mr D Wilkinson on a trip to see a school boys' international football match and staying at Dartmouth as guests of the Royal Navy.

He made attempts to get 4c interested in Poetry with "the burial of Sir John Moore at Corunna" the lines read:

We buried him darkly at dead of night, the sods with our bayonets turning; by the struggling moonbeam's misty light and the lantern dimly burning.

Unfortunately when asked to recite the poem the outcome was:

"They buried him at the dead of night, the sods"

He recalls that the reason for the majority of pegs broken in the cloakroom furniture were due to a bet Alf Lee had when in the Home guard with ex-regulars that he could not progress round the cloakroom without touching the floor. He supported himself by hanging or standing on the pegs and manoeuvring out through the window and back in via the other window swinging on the picture rails and furniture. He won his bet despite breaking the majority of clothes pegs in the process! Mr Lee had a glass eye as a result of an accident when, using a fork to untie his shoe laces, his hand slipped and he stabbed himself in the eye!

Open Day 1956

Mr Holley was involved in a P T Display in the school quadrangle on Parents' Open Day in 1956 and recalls being involved in various Drama plays at the school including "Scuttle booms Treasure".

The following teachers were at Armstrong St School at the closure in July 1964:

Mr Abe, Mr Armstrong, Mr Chadwick, Mr Dixon, Mr Goulding, Mr Holmes, Mr Hollingsworth, Mr Hotchkin, Mr Holley, Mr Holah, Mr Marlborough, Mr Nowell, Mr Smith, Mr Withers, Mr Walker K Tappin A Sapcote and N Robinson.

He recalls that Max Holmes (who had a shop in Victoria St.) would cycle at dinner to the shop to oversee the business and then return back to school for lessons. One day during the afternoon he received a phone call from the shop stating a customer had had his bike stolen from outside it. He promptly went to investigate only to realise he was the culprit as he had come back to school on the customer's bike instead of his own!

He recalls passing a room with total silence and when he entered the class found Mr Goulding sitting on top of a tall cupboard and when asked why he was there stated

"I'm getting a new angle on the class."

Harry Goulding (1942-64)

So it was that one fine Monday morning about the middle of May 1942, full of high hopes I set off on my cycle for the Boys' Department of Armstrong School, some two miles distant. Awaiting me on the steps was the Headmaster, Mr. Harry Horn, a big broad shouldered man with real kindly eyes. He would be in his mid-fifties. A huge smile covered his rubiecund countenance as he greeted me with real warmth and obvious delight, the sort of reception usually accorded to royalty, the only things missing being a fanfare of trumpets and the red carpet. Taking my arm he escorted me up a broad flight of stone steps to the Staff Room where some nine men and four women were busy chatting in small groups or pairs.

"Ladies – Gentlemen, your new colleague: Mr. Goulding- Harry"

"Have we actually come down to taking a St. John's reject?", asked some man, with a loud discordant voice. A great roar of laughter filled the large room with, as far as I could see, only myself not joining in the merriment. Did I detect in the harsh sounding remark a note of hostility? I was soon to find out.

Cleethorpes NUT social, 16th Dec 1953
Back: unknown, Harry Abe, Don Hotchkin, Reg Dixon, Ron Fox, Ken Walker
Seated: Jess Dixon, unknown, unknown, Mrs Hotchkin, Mrs. Walker, Geoff Boyson, Rene Fox, Graham Holley, Brenda Searby, Barbara Holah, Dennis Holah, Elsie Abe

There was just time to be escorted to my classroom No 7 which incidentally was to be my second home without a break for the next three and twenty years. I was handed a little bunch of three keys and told not to attend assembly in the Hall in order to give me a few minutes to find my feet as it were.

Bridges repaired

At the end of the third day I was alone in my room when the door opened to admit one of the senior male members of the staff.

"And what do you reckon you're doing?", he demanded in a voice instantly recognisable as the one heard in the Staff Room on my first arrival.

"Should have thought that was obvious, to anyone possessing the very minimum of hindsight", I replied and went on writing on the Blackboard.

"Look we don't want any St. John's ways at this school."

"That is the very last thing I contemplate doing. I left St. John's last Friday determined never to go near the place again, fully resolved to forget it and all it stands for, so I will thank you not to serve any reminders of what I have put behind me".

"If you make a practice of this sort of thing, we shall all soon be expected to do likewise," he growled.

"You go your way, I'll go mine and I've nothing more to say," I snapped.

The slam of a door told me that the interview, nasty and unpleasant, was over. If he or anyone else for that matter thought that Harry Goulding was the docile submissive, peace at all price type then he or she would quickly come to know differently. Well remember one member of the staff at Armstrong attempting one afternoon to point out the harm done to myself because of my waywardness.

"Harry," he said in kindly tones, "You can at times be most charming but at others you are detestable to a degree".

I make no answer for no one was more aware of my explosive nature than me. On numerous occasions I was told by many different people that the worst enemy I had was none other than myself, but when I eventually came to realise the harm I had done and was still doing it was too late. I am however, pleased to record that the apparent antagonism which showed itself right at the onset of my arrival at Armstrong did not develop in intensity, definitely the reverse. As a matter of fact some four months later when the school was having a "Wings for Victory" Savings Week, of which I organised, my old adversary for the second time entered my den this time accompanied by a lady.

"Harry Goulding" he said to his companion and then to me "My wife".

We shook hands most cordially and then she literally flattered me by turning to her husband and exclaiming "What a lovely smile he has" and most unusual for me I was left speechless. Afterwards I wondered if she had expected to meet some churlish, ill disposed individual for she must have learned a few things not altogether complimentary about me but from that meeting all antagonism twixt Ernie and myself completely evaporated.

When a few years later he developed malignant cancer in the throat our friendship grew. Eventually finding it impossible to eat or drink, he had a tube inserted by which he could take liquid substance but still continued his teaching duties for a time. One day when asked by the sufferer during morning break if I could perform that little feeding task I did so with the utmost willingness. He faced the inevitable with courage and a quiet acceptance that made me feel at times a moral coward.

When eventually he could no longer perform his scholastic duties I was asked by the Headmaster if I felt equal to the task of temporarily taking over some of my stricken colleague's Art classes, about four in all, there being a second teacher of that subject. This was greatly to my liking being chiefly painting in water colours. How I enjoyed those lessons.

I visited Ernie several times and with every successive meeting we drew closer together in the bond of true friendship. His death for me was a sad loss.

Physical training

After 14 years of multi-subject teaching I had no particularly strong preference for any subject or subjects when arriving at Armstrong. Shortly before the end of my first term there, the Headmaster discussed with me the particular sphere or spheres in which he obviously wished me to operate although making no attempt at any compulsion.

"Fancy a bit of PT, Harry?" he asked
"You have a special qualification
in that line of business!"

I leave the reader to guess my immediate response and on receiving my new timetable was overjoyed to find that sixteen periods, mostly during the afternoon sessions, bore the letters P T and the form I was to take. To add to my joy I was placed in full charge of the first and second eleven Soccer teams, the Cricket team and Athletics.

"There will be no interference from anyone but I expect excellent results. Failure to produce such will result in you being replaced," said the Headmaster.

It never came to that for the boys who represented their school did me proud. How well they responded to my insistence for great effort, more effort and still more.

"Good, better, best;
Never let it rest;
Till the good is better
And the better best"

To the boys I must have seemed a man impossible to please for never did I express complete satisfaction with their outstanding achievements. After-match inquests with myself as the coroner were varied. Mistakes on the field of play received strong and caustic disapprobation in full,

whereas anything highly victorious did not receive any comment. I have always been hard that way, it was so with my own son, and not until I was approaching the end of my school sporting activities did I come to realise that a bit of praise is one of the best forms of encouragement to all and sundry and particularly the young.

The sixteen periods on my timetable which had been allotted to Physical Training could be carried out in the big school yard, the rather small gymnasium or the inner grass quadrangle. While the weather continued warm and dry I decided to operate in the last mentioned area, of which I will, for a certain reason, give a rough plan.

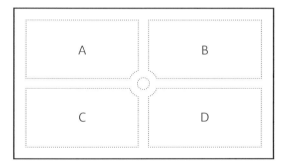

Girls' school

The incident I am about to relate took place on the very first day of our return to work after the long summer vacation of 1942 when the whole of every afternoon for me was P T. The table of exercises involving arm, leg, balance, dorsal, was performed on grass plot A, but when it came to the four different team activities I naturally made use of all four rectangular plots. Thus Greens operated in A, Yellows in B, Blues in D and Reds in C. After some 4 minutes or so I blew the whistle upon which the four teams moved around thus A to B, B to D, D to C, C to A. This was repeated until the full circuit was completed, thus bringing an enjoyable lesson in which I had fully participated to a highly satisfactory conclusion, or at least I thought so.

"Now what's up?" I asked myself, instinct warning as if something was amiss as I beheld a tall, pale-faced stately female of some fifty summers or thereabouts, making her way towards me. Reckon she goes to London for her corset, I thought. In a couple of ticks I'm going to be the modest recipient of hearty congratulations on a sterling performance of great merit though she doesn't look altogether too pleased. Still I braced myself to receive graciously her plaudits, acting with due decorum and becoming modesty.

"Good afternoon Mr - er - er"

"Goulding" I interposed, and a wee anxious to be friendly, sociable and above all so helpful by spelling the word.

"Thank you but I don't need a spelling lesson. Will you in future refrain from using that side of the quadrangle which happens to be part of MY school? Your boys charging about greatly distract my girls at their lessons. Kindly continue all activities in the future to your own half."

Her reproof duly administered she retraced her steps in the best possible regal style walking across our half of the quadrangle towards the far door from which she had emerged.

I shall never know how I stopped myself from shouting after her, "Hey! You're on our half" and furthermore where she could put her 50% of the green turf, flagstones and all.

When later the Headmaster who had witnessed the interview from his room overlooking the quadrangle, and somehow guessed all was not right, mentioned the matter and I told him, expressing my thorough disgust.

"Don't upset yourself, Harry," he smilingly replied "best keep to our side in future."

For some six years I greatly enjoyed PT lessons, games and athletics and then it was curtains, for when approaching forty years of age I started putting on weight in alarming fashion. Such things as handstands, vaulting, somersaults, leaps and jumps could not be performed as of old. Muscle was running to fat and the Headmaster was not slow to notice my decline and act accordingly.

"I'm taking you off PT Harry. Fancy a bit of RI (Religious Instruction)"

I needed no persuasion to change, for carrying some fourteen stones in the gymnasium was proving a real burden. At the same time I was given a share in the teaching of mathematics, though in a somewhat junior capacity. Mr Cyril Bristow taught the "A" forms, Mr Ricketts the "B1" stream. I found myself with the "B2" stars.

Conflict at school

Although most warmly welcomed by the Headmaster, Mr Harry Horn, it was almost immediately apparent that at least two of my new colleagues took exception to my arrival and for one particular reason in that I hailed from St. John's Church of England School. In patently sarcastic manner I was referred to as "The bishop" or "Rev" and once by mistake as "Archbishop". To such similar cheap gibes I always remained outwardly calm and unruffled and, if any reader think that such remarks were made in a joking manner I must emphasise that such was obviously not so. One individual some ten years my senior, never lost an opportunity in belittling me and always within the hearing of a good audience in the large Staff Room.

About the middle of 1943, the staff including four married ladies was reinforced by the arrival of a very young man to whom I shall refer by his Christian name - Charles. Tall, very slender, pale faced and wearing glasses he at once as I had, two years previously, demonstrated his keenness to do everything within his powers to further the interests of the school, and like myself, became the object of ridicule from certain quarters. Returning to school one day after lunch I learned from more than one source of a brief encounter between poor Charles and the mighty muscleman. It was I understood a floor where he suffered the indignity of having his shoes and socks removed and thrown by his adversary through an open window to the inner grass quadrangle some fifteen feet or so below, causing no end of hilarity to the spectators in the Staff Room.

The news infuriated me and I made no secret of the fact that I ardently wished it had been done to myself and not Charles and he picks his men all right but takes good care to side track me and I'm sure always will. Never for one moment did I imagine that a showdown would ever come about twixt "Atlas" and myself. I never sought one and inwardly hoped that such would never happen and then quite unexpectedly it all did.

One afternoon during the break lasting from 2.45 to 3.00pm I made my way to the Staff Room being as usual one of the last to arrive and here let me emphasise I did not resort to sup tea, smoke or do both. Actually I went in deference to the Headmasters wishes. Not long after my arrival at Armstrong I ceased going in the Staff Room preferring to keep to my form room. This was speedily noticed by Mr. Horn who in most kindly fashion asked if I would be a little more sociable. After telling him that I regretted one or two of the staff were no more sociable to me he placed a hand on my shoulder adding "I won't press the matter, Harry, but I do not like any divisions on my staff". So from time to time I made odd appearances when childish utterances such as "Are you a member of staff?" would be made, such remarks were generally made light heartedly to be treated as such, but not always.

"Atlas" was standing with his broad backside to the fire leaving but a narrow space between himself and the large table for me to pass. As he was holding a cup of tea and chatting to one of the oldest members of the staff, I took great pains to turn sideways so to edge past him. I need not have bothered. Suddenly he dropped the cup, showering all the contents down the front of my clothing, particularly the fly of my trousers. I would by a great amount of will power have been prepared to accept an expression of regret on his part until he loudly guffawed followed by a cry "look he's wet himself." That remark did it, for I responded in a manner he never expected. On the table

right to hand was a tray on which two full cups of tea, not up to then claimed, rested. In a flash I seized one and threw the entire contents in like manner down him adding "And you take that ye'r bugger".

That did it, with his face contorted with rage and blind fury he hissed,

"Just come over here and I'll teach you a bloody lesson".

Without another word on either side or no attempt at conciliation by anybody present I followed him to one end of the room where there was plenty of open floor space. Before I had time to remove my jacket and roll up my shirt sleeves, battle commenced. A sudden and completely unexpected rush on the part of my adversary, took me completely by surprise as I found myself in a vice-like grip and quite unable to move my arms. For the next couple of minutes there was a desperate struggle as he strove might and main to put me on the deck! I needed every possible ounce of strength to foil him, and let me confess it was only by a very narrow margin that I was able to do so. When he tried to lift me bodily off my feet I countered by pressing downwards. Never in my life had I been so hard pressed, not even when "Smokey Joe" chased me all around the ring. I waited for his grip to relax and when it did wrenched my arms free, seized him round the neck and forced his head backwards. In a matter of moments he was off balance and lying on his back on the floor with thirteen and a half stones on top of him. Still gripping him round the throat I dug my thumbs in savagely. He ceased to struggle as his face became redder and redder and though completely at my mercy, I was in no mood to release him. It was only when I heard someone say "That will do Harry. You've won" that I consented to release him. He was assisted to his feet, and seated in a chair to recover. With mixed feelings I promptly left the room, pleased with the result and yet dissatisfied. On the one hand I had given HIM a lesson that he would not forget in a hurry but on the other, had not removed his shoes and socks and thrown them on the school roof.

Teaching methods

Teaching techniques vary widely in the which I had my own particular brand. My unorthodox methods in Mathematics were the cause of great amusement to my colleagues and always new boys not acquainted. One of my favourites was to sing, for example, some new mathematical formula such as "Volume of a sphere equals 4πr3 divided by 3" in a rich baritone voice.

One poor misguided specimen observed "Sir, you ought to make a record." I would reply "Of course, I will. Come out," and when he did so promptly seized him and bent him over a desk and held my cane up in the air. Brandishing it fiendishly like a knobkerrie, above the upturned little bottom of the facetious pupil I would exclaim:

"I will now administer a RECORD number of strokes"; which of course did not take place. What a brand of classroom humour!

Acheivers

Armstrong Secondary Modern School was the academy where boys and girls who had failed the 11+ were admitted to continue their schooling and every September a fresh intake of some 150 boys produced two or three outstanding boys, intellectually that is. I would scratch my head and wonder how in the name of heaven such had failed to make the grade. Fortunately for such unfortunates all was not lost, for, because of a wise scheme such highly promising material known as "late developers" could be transferred to the Grammar School or Technical College. I well remember one such boy when I was responsible for the A stream Mathematics for which he showed real aptitude. For once I found myself murmuring "He'll make a Maths man." So off to the Grammar School he went, much to my joy and great satisfaction.

Some five years later he came to see me just when I was vociferously hammering

home some Mathematical principle. With a faint smile he stood for a few moments surveying a familiar scene before I advanced to greet him.

"Nothing changes," he said smiling.

"Wrong!" I replied. "Kids get worse and worse."

"If I remember rightly, sir, that is what you so often told us when I sat in that seat in fear and trembling," he said, pointing to a certain desk. Then he informed me that he was going to University to read Mathematics.

"How did you come to choose that particular branch of learning?" I enquired.

"Well sir, I owe it to you for when at this school I developed a great liking for your subject". That was a real shot in the arm for me and I was even more delighted when some three years later he re-appeared to tell me that he had gained a second class honours Degree.

Mistaken identity

Of a particular experience I once greatly enjoyed. One evening I attended a function at which many of the Town's celebrities were present including the Chairman of the local Education Committee who eventually entered into conversation with me. I knew him of course, but was a complete stranger to him. After shaking hands and introducing ourselves he eventually enquired as to what I did for a living.

"I am employed by the committee of which you are chairman," was my response, without giving any details.

"Ah" he exclaimed somewhat excitedly, "You will be one of our school CARETAKERS", and when I smiled as if in acknowledgement, added "through long experience of meeting and talking with people acquired a sort of sixth sense by which I can pinpoint their occupations".

How I held a straight face I shall never know. Having demonstrated his uncanny ability in one particular direction he naturally did not wish to be seen in long and earnest conversation with a school caretaker of all people so with the meaningless "Pleased to have met you" and a lukewarm handshake he scuttled off doubtless thinking "Definitely the brush & shovel type- stamped all over him". But how long had you been teaching? One might well ask. Only a mere thirty years.

Music

Just after the end of the Second World War a Mr W R Leafe LRAM joined the staff at Armstrong Boys' School. He was indeed a most valuable acquisition as proof of which the following details relating to his achievements must surely testify. Slightly older than myself he had taught for some twenty years in a Cleethorpes junior school with competence. A talented musician, he also did some very good work in the field of drama. When I add that he founded the Cleethorpes String Orchestra (C S O) with some thirty-five performers, put the Grimsby Music Festival firmly on its feet, and successfully organised the combined schools' Christmas carol concert at the large Central Hall in Grimsby it will be realised what a powerful influence he executed in the musical life in the district.

At Armstrong School I would say that, like myself, he was not welcomed with open arms, so I suppose it was not altogether surprising that Roland and I quickly established a happy mutual understanding. Life for Roland in the Staff Room was not easy in that he was a victim of ever-increasing deafness and though possessing a hearing aid was often unable to follow conversation. I well remember him telling me one day how he found it most disconcerting to be in a group, a silent witness as it were, and particularly so when all around him would suddenly roar with laughter at some witticism, ribald remark, or even possibly an obscenity, not one word of which he had heard. "I laugh with them in an artificial way," he once confessed to me, "but I feel out of it." When however, he followed that up by telling me that even without his hearing

aid he'd never had the slightest difficulty in hearing what I said, I was overjoyed because I never shouted or raised my voice when conversing with him though I do freely admit to possessing what is known as a 'carrying voice' as to which my wife will readily concur.

But I must return post-haste to Roland, who in a very short space of time formed a fine school choir and trained some excellent vocal soloists. They were quickly in great demand, going as far as Louth, some sixteen miles away, to entertain, in the course of which I often went as company for Roland and as general help.

Then he asked if I would act as a sort of general factotum in the running of his popular String Orchestra. I was only too willing to assist in any way possible. So every Friday night saw me pedalling off to Mill Road Methodist Chapel at the far end of Cleethorpes to assist at the weekly rehearsal which proved most enjoyable with all the players being so friendly. One of my duties was the distribution and collection of the music - a keeper of the music, as some would have it. It was also my duty to set up and put away the music stands as well as superintend the tea arrangements halfway through the practice. The chapel was some three miles from our house, but whatever the weather, and it can be very severe during the winter on the east coast, I never failed to be at my post of duty.

It was a sad day for me when Roland, bitterly disillusioned as regards lack of recognition of his great musical expertise at Armstrong School, returned to resume teaching in his own home town of Cleethorpes though our happy association as regards the CSO suffered in no way at all, but sad to relate the end was only just around the corner.

Fire drill

When a new Headmaster one day arrived at Armstrong School he quickly decided to make his presence felt and show his worth by introducing certain ideas hitherto quite foreign to me for one.

"The school must learn how to act with the utmost speed, efficiency and calmness in case of Fire", he announced to a hushed audience at the conclusion of Assembly one morning. "I want to see how expeditiously this school building can be evacuated in case of a sudden emergency. The clanging of the school bell will serve as the alarm."

Back in our form room I carefully explained to my devoted little band of fourteen year olds not renowned for intelligence of what it was all about. "One day, I cannot tell you exactly when, this school will be on fire" I said with all due solemnity which brought looks of genuine joy to the faces of all my hearers. "You won't laugh on waking up to find yourself, a little mound of ash" I warned, upon which the smiles vanished twice as quickly as when appearing. "Evacuation does not mean a mass visit to the toilets or that we all gallop off home. With the flames licking round us there will be no panic or any sign of terror. Like well trained soldiers we shall calmly proceed to safety and just remember that we cannot all be first to do so."

Now it was just a question of waiting to spring into action when the school rapidly became a blazing inferno with acrid fumes and dense blinding, choking smoke testing our ... to the very limit of human endurance, but day after day passed without anything untoward happening until nearly everybody including myself had been well and truly lulled into a state of false security. Then quite unexpectedly one morning when my room was as quiet as a morgue the silence was shattered by a continuous deafening clanging of the school hand bell.

"This can't possibly be the end of this lesson period", I thought to myself. To every boy who had stopped work and was staring at me as if paralysed, I snapped "Get on with your work – never heard a bell ringing?"

"Please, sir" spoke one alert specimen rising in his seat, "p'p'please sir, school's on fire."

"I know that", I said sniffing, "Thought I could detect burning. Stop work

and prepare to evacuate".

Opening the classroom door, facing a long corridor which led to the school yard, I found a barricade had been quietly and craftily erected bearing a large notice which read "The fire is here!!" which meant no evacuation was possible along the corridor. That left only one escape route leading to the school yard. At the far end of the classroom were some half a dozen small windows each about eighteen inches square which could be quickly opened to hang downwards I opened one and promptly slithered out feet first into safety. Quickly opening the other windows the boys swiftly followed my shining example demonstrating to the Headmaster standing stop watch in hand in the yard how expeditiously Room 7 had been evacuated with no loss of life or a single casualty of any description. Later he discussed with me our brilliant performance.

"Very good work, Mr Goulding, with but one criticism, It should be boys first- teacher last, whereas," he smiled, "It was the reverse!"

It was my turn to smile on replying "And when the good shepherd pulleth forth his sheep, he goes before them and the sheep follow him for they know his voice", adding that those words to me drew a very striking picture of the loving, caring and trustful relationship between the faithful teacher and his little flock. He goes before them not only teaching encouragement and mildly admonishing but also by example showing them the way. They follow, recognising the loving tender voice which so often speaks kind words of help and inspiration. Then looking at the recently appointed Head I added, "But a stranger will they not follow."

Subsidence

Of far more importance was the condition of the building which was giving cause for grave concern. Within ten years of construction ominous cracks began to appear in both inner and outer walls which, as time went by, rapidly became longer and ever wider. In my own form room I could quite easily insert my hand in one such fissure. Huge baulks of timber were leaned against the outer walls where the building was double storeyed to act as props and supports. From time to time building inspectors and surveyors appeared on the scene to examine and make recommendations.

After one such visit the Headmaster informed me that I was no longer to take any Physical Training in the hall which served as a gymnasium as forty boys together with a heavy weight instructor performing vigorous activities usually in unison was highly dangerous; just as the walls of Jericho had collapsed, merely by vocal sound waves so too and even more easily could the walls of Armstrong School tremble and crash to earth under the impact of leap frog, skip jumping and the like. It was a truly frightening prospect as the latest in a long line of inspectors of Public Works & Buildings had stated in his report,

A few years later two or three men arrived and started boring deep holes about six inches in diameter at carefully fixed spots just outside the outer walls. I was greatly interested and soon learned that a solid chalk base had been reached at a depth of some ninety feet (I cannot remember the exact figure). The sunken piles had in some cases not been firmly bottomed and, to make matters worse, certain piles could not ever be found. Consequently serious subsidence had resulted. Armstrong School was doomed, which saddened me not a little.

Books on display

To strike a more serious note, one morning when preparations were being made for the super turnout on display in the afternoon, a boy, almost breathless burst into my form room, "Mr – (the headmaster at the time) says will you send three English work books from your form 4d to be put on display". I duly complied, carefully selecting the very best, an average book and the very worst which was a real shocker. Less than 2 minutes later, I found myself facing the headmaster who looked as if any second he would have

an epileptic fit. In a voice pulsating with uncontrolled bad temper he demanded to know why I had the effrontery to send such a sample, knowing full well that what he required where the three best books. "Do you expect me to put this on view?" he demanded, his voice shaking with passion.

"Those books represent a true cross-section of the written English done in this form. The worst book demonstrates to "the man on the street" that class teaching is very far from being the easy job it is so often made out to be. I suppose you do know that teaching backward pupils is far more demanding and difficult than dealing with pupils such as are found in our A stream". He promptly cut the discussion short. "I want the three best books", he snapped and scuttled out.

His Majesty's Inspectors

When first starting my teaching career the headmaster gave me a bit of sound advice namely to keep my cane well out of sight should an Inspector be prowling around. I dutifully obeyed but as is so often the case, my vigilance gradually lessened with the inevitable result.

My delightfully informal welcome and introductions having been made one fine morning, our visitor promptly made a dive for the two class registers lying on my little desk. It was quite impossible to perform any super vanishing trick as pointing to the miserable weapon lying in full view he asked in a most horrified voice "What is this?"

I picked it up tenderly, almost lovingly as if I had found something precious that had been missing for over a month. "Ah" I replied, "Its uses are indeed quite multi-factious to be sure. This, my baton when conducting hymn singing and the rendering of songs in music lessons," I paused.

"And what else?"

"Oh! It is most useful when acting as a pointer during geography lessons when boys fix their full attention on the big wall maps in use."

"Is that all?"

"Oh far from it", I replied. "Caught a mouse with it a short time ago. Rather unwise of it to take up lodgings in my cupboard, don't you think?"

"It looks to me, suspiciously like a cane", he replied in a really meaningful manner but I was not one to capitulate tamely.

"A cane!!!" I repeated in a tone of sheer disbelief. "It may resemble such a thing but at certain times I prefer to use my tongue, always kept to razor edge sharpness".

"I see", he said, replacing my last line of defence on the table. Thank God canes don't talk, I thought to myself, at the same time casting serious doubts as to whether I had acted like a first-class convincing liar. At this very moment I have the gravest doubts. Here I will say that when from time to time I have found myself in tight situations I wriggle to safety usually in one of two ways, either by talking my way out or muddling through in some sort of fashion.

Illness of staff member

Sometime in the early 50s, something most unexpected occurred one morning at Armstrong School. Morning assembly had just concluded and forms were preparing to start another day's instruction when a boy burst into room seven where I was just about to go into action, to tell me that the headmaster wished to see me immediately. At once I tried to think what the urgent summons was all about. What could be amiss relating doubtless to myself? I turned to the form I was about to teach, set them to work and followed my caller, the very acme of urgency and impatience. Soon a strange and completely unexpected sight met my gaze for their stretched out on the floor and quite motionless lay my old adversary whom I had once engaged in a trial of strength and worsted. I stared downwards in nonchalant style until the voice of the headmaster told me why I had been summoned.

"Mr Goulding, would you help to take him to my room?" But I needed no help in slinging him over my right shoulder. I carried some 12 stones of deadweight up a flight of 20 stone stairs to his destination, to drop him none too gently in a chair. At the time I was a strong man, some 15 stones in weight when stripped, and well used to carrying 16 stone sacks of corn, so the burden was well within my compass but to my amusement the headmaster more than once in the future referred to my "strong man act".

"Thank you, Mr Goulding", I heard him say as I hastened out of the room, sorry - should have written "study" - and fair flew down the stairs to my room or rather scene of operations where far more important things needed my full attention.

I believe it was a coronary thrombosis but was far too disinterested to make any enquiries - though I did learn he had been rushed to hospital which meant I would almost certainly have to take some of his lessons, the mere thought of which highly displeased me.

A fortnight later, whilst on my way to evening school, I decided for no really valid reason to call in and see him. The ward sister, most officious as befitted her high station, but obviously impressed by my manly bearing and gentlemanly ways, readily gave me permission to pay my "courtesy call" before the official visiting time.

"I never expected to see you", was the greeting from my arch enemy.

"Heard you were critical so have come before it's too late!"

"Oh! I'm not as bad as all that. Improving nicely as a matter of fact".

"Went in the mortuary first", I replied. "Thought you might be there, still there's plenty of time for that."

"How's night school going?" he asked. anxious to change the unwholesome nature of my conversation. He was actually the warden in charge of the Institute.

"Great!" I replied. "Things have certainly gone much better during your absence."

I left him after asking if he had any strong views about floral tributes: "buttercups, daisies and dandelions go well together," I added before taking my leave.

New intake

After a couple of years, Dixon requested the headmaster to relieve him of Mathematics, saying that he found it too demanding particularly in view of his health. He had some sort of back trouble and was often absent or forced to rest in the Staff Room. To make things much easier for him he was given a share in the teaching of History but strange to say, kept his post as a Gardening Specialist doubtless in view of the fact that it was a post of special responsibility worth an extra £50 per annum.

His place was taken by young teacher, Mr Wilkinson by name, who had just graduated in Mathematics at Nottingham University. He quickly settled in, proving himself to be a decided acquisition. Together we formed a formidable team that seemed to go from strength to strength as the years went by but, as is so often the case, circumstances changed almost overnight.

New headmaster

The commencement of the summer term 1955 saw our caretaker head, sitting like Caesar on his throne, the big difference being that like some potentate or chief he merely squatted on a long three legged stool, in front of which I was never to be seen paying homage on bended knee. All too soon though I was left in no doubt that our "caretaker head", was, as regards myself, preparing to wreak vengeance.

On several occasions he entered my room and, ignoring me completely, walked around, scrutinising the mathematics done by the boys the which I heartily welcomed knowing full well that such would stand up to the closest inspection. It was noticeable that not once did he ever time his visit to

coincide with when I was actually giving a lesson, all very carefully planned me thought. In vain I waited for him as a matter of common courtesy to discuss the purpose of his visit as if such was not apparent. Surreptitiously he crept in and just as stealthily crawled out, dirty work was in progress sure enough but though I prepared to take a vicious low punch I never for some unaccountable reason envisaged a knife being plunged into my back.

After the long summer vacation I returned to work to learn from certain members of the staff that I was no longer Head of the Mathematics Department. I was the very last person on the staff to learn of my kick out. Here I must place on record my sincere thanks to those members of the staff who made it their business to come to my room and express their well meant sympathy.

I have no doubt that my case would have been strengthened had I been a member of the N A S or even the N U T but this was not the case. I had allowed my membership of the latter union to lapse many years earlier.

In place of teaching Mathematics, I was promptly switched to Gardening. Strange as it may seem but quite obvious to me, it promptly ceased to be a post of special responsibility as it had been when Dixon "ruled the clods".

The new caretaker head vacated the position of warden of the Armstrong Evening Institute, and needless to say, I was not given the appointment despite my seniority in age and 25 years of continuous evening school teaching, the latter of which no teacher at Armstrong could equal.

At the annual School Sports I had three years officiated as Starter. I was promptly relieved of that post being relegated unceremoniously to the status of controlling the spectators who far outnumbered the competitors, but almost unbelievably I was graciously permitted to retain my post as Form Master of the most difficult class in the school, known as 4D, comprising school leavers of the lowest intelligence plus a goodly selection of delinquents from the Remand Home. So successful was I in that capacity that nobody ever dreamed of giving me change.

On going to Armstrong in 1942 I was put in charge of form 3D in room seven and in 1964 when the school finally closed its doors I was still in room seven controlling form 4D, the difference in the form group coming about through the school leaving age being raised from 14 years to 15 years.

I was in charge of form 4D reputed to be the most difficult bunch in the school and consequently needed a strong teacher. Actually it never turned out that way, for nearly all were good, down-to-earth material, the type with which I had been associated in my boyhood days. I understood them well and they in turn were not slow to realise my firm but sympathetic approach. Unfortunately such lads are often all too easily led with the result that the odd one or two occasionally found themselves in trouble with the police the which usually happened within two years of leaving school.

Staff photographs

From time to time a professional photographer would appear to take beautiful pictures sometimes in glorious Technicolor of every scholar, the school football teams, most wonderful of all a staff photograph, with the headmaster perched in the middle of the front row with three or four senior members of the staff likewise seated at each side, all, with the exception of one having the right leg beautifully crossed over the left.

The non-descript stood at the rear. It was as I remarked to John, my best friend and colleague, a simple business of "cream in the front, skimmed milk at the back" to which John merely asked, "and who's in the third row out of focus?"

"John and Harry of course!". Shaking heads we there and then decided to go missing.

The very next morning I saw from my form room window a few chairs set out in the inner quadrangle, a beautiful stretch of turf and at the mid-morning break the staff collecting thereon, some adjusting their ties, others attending to their coiffure in a somewhat vain attempt to look like some handsome film stars. "Never was so much brain assembled at such short notice in so small an area," I murmur to myself, and laughed outright.

My door flies open as a prefect gasping for breath rushes in "P-please, sir, the headmaster says, will you come for the photograph?"

"Why! You're out of breath a boy. You mustn't rush about like that. Now return at walking pace and tell him you have delivered the message".

A few seconds pass and he reappears with an even more urgent request for my attendance which this time is completely ignored.

The door opens a third time to reveal me doing some sketches in colour on the blackboard. I do not turn my head when I hear the voice of my esteemed headmaster for I am most particular as to the correct order of my priorities. I guess he is finding it extremely difficult to control his feelings.

"Will you come at once for the staff photograph? The photographer has a lot to do".

Sadly I shake my head at the same time adding "and so have I", before turning my back and resuming my artistic efforts.

The classroom door slams to violently and a few seconds later a picture of some of the staff is duly taken, not one of whom will ever be able to say "that's Harry Goulding, don't know what happened to him. Probably dead by now". Which all goes to prove...?

Headmaster appointment

It was almost the unanimous belief of the staff at Armstrong that when "Chopper" retired in 1962 he will be succeeded by his close bosom friend none other than Dixon. There is an old saying, "Birds of a feather flock together", and Dixon indeed to me was a perfect replica of his predecessor. They were both staunch advocates of N U T policy and as such often hostile to people like myself who preferred not to join. My father, an honest hard-working man never joined any trade union and for most of my professional career I did likewise, having strong objections to being told when I was not to go to work by some executive body and furthermore when I was to resume my duties. To go on strike was abhorrent to me.

I was senior to Dixon both in age and teaching experience but that did not prevent his childish taunt always in the hearing of others, being loudly expressed. "Now Bishop!" he would proclaim, a reference to the fact that I taught Divinity.

So, no one was the least surprised when Dixon succeeded "Chopper" to rule for a couple of years ere the demolition squad moved in. As for myself the situation remained unchanged, beyond the fact he ceased referring to me as "Bishop" which was only to be expected seeing that during the first 12 months of his regime we had but one brief conversation lasting about 15 seconds.

During the second and final year, really close harmony began to avail with no less than three very short conversations taking place. Apart from those we remained poles apart.

Sports day

I believe it was during Chopper's reign that another wonderful idea came from the fertile mind of some teacher. It had always been the custom for the Girls' and Boys' Departments to hold their respective Sports Day quite independently until it was discovered one great day that the two departments were indeed one school and should function as such, at least in the playing field. When I pointed out that the two full programs could not possibly be carried through in one afternoon I was speedily overruled and combined Ops came into being. This leads me to what happened one glorious afternoon in July when nearly 1000 girls and boys, some 40 teachers plus Dixon and his female counterpart found themselves in close harmony, with the female section fluttering around like gaily painted butterflies and their male counterparts resembling a small army of crows.

All went well for about an hour at which stage the boy in excited tones informed me that two drunken men had come on the scene. Actually they were some 20 yards behind the spectators lining one long side of the oval running track. Now and again each quenched his thirst from a large bottle but neither appeared obstreperous in any way. Although my close friend John and I were spectators' stewards I never considered it our duty to keep the adult section plus a couple of slightly inebriated young men under strict control. Then quite unexpectedly it all happened. Hearing a bit of a commotion I looked around to see our two characters hastening towards where the two Heads were seated surrounded by some 25 officials of one sort or another, positioned some hundred yards away from where I was standing. At that distance it was impossible to know what was said but suddenly two young teachers tackled the more domineering of the two interlopers and with that we were treated to the spectacle of three men rolling over and over the ground with legs and arms flying in all directions. It was just the sort of thing 900 senior boys and girls wanted as shrieks of laughter and yells of delight rose all around. I fair groaned that two supposedly educated men should demean themselves thus and to make matters worse in full view of the public gaze. Here however I must give full marks to the acting headmistress who promptly decided that she, her staff and every girl should quit the battlefield at once. The loud cheering from some 400 boys announced the arrival of the "arm of the law" in the shape of two constables who quietly and effectively escorted our two intruders from the scene. Thus the afternoon came to a premature close though it was not finality as far as John and I were concerned.

On the following day Friday, just as the afternoon session was about to begin, a prefect entered my room to inform me that my presence was required in Dixon's room; I needed no one to tell me the purpose of my visit.

"No need to hurry, Harry boy", said I to myself as I leisurely made up the register for the week including the percentage attendance and the number of attendances made by every boy, after which I casually sauntered to the meeting place.

At the foot of the stairs I met John who discussed with me our plan of campaign before facing the Inquisition.

As fully expected, Dixon at once placed all the blame for what had happened the previous afternoon fairly and squarely on our shoulders. Had we done our rightful duty as spectators' stewards nothing untoward in the slightest would have happened. We were totally to blame. I could have laughed outright but in silence allowed him complete his castigation before giving him the "works". There was no need for a disgusting exhibition of pure animal behaviour on the part of two male teachers towards a person however objectionable. The approach was completely wrong, John and I did not believe in brawling especially in the view of hundreds of children and we preferred to use a bit of psychology or, as I prefer to put

it, exercise a little common sense. So ended a delightful little tête-à-tête with my superior in office but certainly not in anything else.

Final day at Armstrong

Two days later it was end of term with Armstrong closing its doors for the last time. I never went in the Staff Room so have no idea what took place there. Close to the school was the River Freshney but "by the waters of Freshney" I did not "sit down and weep".

When for the last time the school bell rang, I dismissed my form, wiped clean the blackboards and then sat at my desk. For over 23 years I had laboured hard in room seven. The end of an era in my life had come, it was time to turn pastures new but at most it could only be for seven years.

About 4.30pm I decided to make my final exit. Gathering a few personal possessions I wheeled my cycle out of the room where it had always been parked for the last 20 years and proceeded down the deserted, corridor to the main entrance. Propping my cycle against the outside wall, I turned to make my way up the stone staircase to the Staff Room, the headmaster's "STUDY", The secretary's office and the staff loo, the last place of which I duly patronised. All were deserted. My visit concluded with a short visit to the study, where five successive heads had reigned in glory, honour, might and majesty. Seating myself in the luxurious, comfortable, armchair, closed my eyes and allowed my mind to wander freely and for some 5 min. Then rising to my feet I shouted,

"Ichabod - Ichabod"

And as the sound reverberated through the building deserted, save for the very oldest of its final occupants, I retraced my steps, rode my cycle once around the big school yard, thence into Armstrong Street and so home, along the route I had traversed so many thousands of times while over and over again I repeated those well-known lines of Christina Georgina Rossetti which I had memorised when a boy at the grammar school.

"Better by far you should forget and smile

Than that you should remember and be sad."

Have I forgotten? The answer
is obviously, "not quite".

Footnote

Mr. Harry Goulding wrote his memoirs of
his life in approx 1979 and these extracts
are from his working life at Armstrong
School (1942 – 1964). They have been
taken from hand written copies submitted
by his grandson, Peter Goulding, who has
kindly allowed them to be reproduced.

© M Foster-Smith

*50 years on there is little evidence that a school ever existed
on the site save for the railings which surround it.*

Headmasters

**Frederick Barnard
Potter**
1929-1938

Harry Horn
1938-1948

John Holmes
1948-1956

Alfred Lawrence Lee
1956-1962

George Reginald Dixon
1962-1964

Register of teaching staff

NAME	BORN	START DATE	FINISH DATE	NOTES
Harry Abe	1906	Nov 1929	July 1964 *	- from Strand St School
Charles H Allison	1873	1932	Jan 1938	- Resigned
John Nicholas Armstrong	1913	Jan 1938	July 1964 *	- War service 1940-1946
D H Armstrong		July 1963		
D Bateson		Jan 1948	Dec 1948	
Alfred Beales	1907	Sept 1929 *	July 1935	- to Edward St Boys School
J Blackburn		Sept 1961	Sept 1962	
Cyril Harper Bristow	1889	Sept 1929 *	Aug 1944	- to Holme Hill School as Headmaster
Harold Brooks	1907	Sept 1936	Sept 1938	- Transfer to South Parade
G R Boyson		Sept 1953	July 1956	
J Canning		Mar 1949	Mar 1949	- Did not take up his duties
T J Chadwick	1931	Sept 1954	Sept 1962	- Tranfer to Armstrong Girls
C H Chapman		July 1946	Mar 1947	- Transfer to Nunsthorpe
P C Chessman		Oct 1947	Jan 1948	
Mrs E T Cleave		Sept 1951	Part time 1956	
W G Cole		Nov 1948	Mar 1949	
C H Coleman		Aug 1948	Apl 1952	
George Thomas Cressey		Apl 1947	Dec 1947	
R Cusack			July 1959	
D Davy		Sep 1963		
N Dearden		Aug 1940	May 1949	- War service 1942-1946 - to Holme Hill School as Headmaster
Norman Walter Dingley	1904	Apr 1930	May 1941	
George Reginald Dixon	1908	Sept 1938	July 1964 *	- from Victoria St. Boys - War service 1941-1946 - Headmaster 1962-1964
L Driver		Feb 1959	Sept 1961	
B A Elvin		Oct 1961	June 1963	
F A Everett		Sep 1963		
J Evison		Sept 1962	July 1964*	
J Farrow		Aug 1930	Sep 1933	- to Nunsthorpe
C A Forde		Sept 1948	Aug 1950	- to Home Office Service
Ronald Fox	1916	Sept 1939	July 1956	- War service 1940-1946
E C Fuller		Sept 1938	Aug 1948	- from South Parade S Boys
Albert H Goulding	1905	May 1942	July 1964*	- from St. Johns
R W Gravels		Sept 1963		- from Scartho Primary
J M Gregory		June 1949	July 1952	- to Holme Hill
Walter Harriman	1909	June 1934	Sept 1938	- to Victoria St. Boys
C E Hayes		May 1943	Aug 1950	- to Scartho
Cecil T Herbert	1918	Jan 1948	Nov 1952	- to Nunsthorpe
Thomas Charles Huggins	1907	Sept 1929 *	March 1930	- to Holme Hill
Frederick Henry Hodgson	1906	Sept 1935	May 1936	- to Scartho
John Dennis Holah	1930	July 1952	July 1964 *	
Graham Holley	1930	July 1952	July 1964 *	
William D Hollingsworth	1909	Sept 1938	July 1964 *	- War service 1942-1945
Harry Horn		Aug 1938	Retired Aug 1948	- from South Parade - Headmaster 1938–1948
John Holmes	1910	Sept 1948	April 1956	- to Beacon Hill School - Headmaster 1948–1956
Maxey M Holmes	1908	1937	July 1964 *	- from Holme Hill School - War Service 1941- 1946
Leslie Alfred Hoose	1929	July 1952	Dec 1953	
Donald A Hotchkin	1916	Dec 1946	July 1964 *	
Albert Alan Hopkinson	1926	Sept 1951	Sept 1955	- to Isle of Wight

NAME	BORN	START DATE	FINISH DATE	NOTES
Thomas .W Johnson		Sep 1938	Jan 1939	
S W Kay		Aug 1942	Sept 1944	- to Frode as Headmaster
Mr Knowles				
James Henry Kew	1881	Sept 1929 *	Nov 1946	- Retired
Mr Lancaster				
W R Leafe		Sept 1944	Aug 1948	
Alec Bennet Leake	1901	Feb 1931	Dec 1951	- to Elliston St School
Alfred Lawrence Lee	1898	Sept. 1938	Retired 1962	- from South Parade - Headmaster Sept 1956-1962
S Marchant		Sept 1950	Sept 1951	- to Nigeria
Geoffrey F Marleborough	1910	Sept 1938	July 1964 *	- War service 1940-1946
Wilfred Hugh Mᶜ Crohan	1906	March 1930	Feb 1931	- to Edward St Boys School
Wilfred Hugh Mᶜ Crohan	1906	Sept 1959		- from Victoria St Boys School
C W Merry		Aug 1942	July 1946	- to Welhome school
David Alan Nowell	1900	Sept 1938	July 1964 *	- from South Parade - p/t from Jan 1963
B Pedley		Sep 1963		
Leslie O Peters	1919	Sept 1950	April 1953	- to Woodhall Spa
M J Phillipson		Sep 1963		
Frederick Barnard Potter	1877	Sept 1929 *	Retired Aug 1938	- Headmaster 1929-1938
Harry Ernest Potts	1911	Oct 1931	Sept 1938	- to Nunsthorpe Senior Mixed
Cyril. F Ricketts		Aug 1938	June 1943	- to & from Edward St Boys
Neil Robinson		Sept 1963	1964	
Austin Sapcote		Sept 1963	June 1963	
A I Sharp		Sept 1962	Oct 1963	- to Western Boys
M D Shaw		Sept 1958	Sept 1961	
John James Sigley	1915	Sept 1935	August 1937	- Died
Kenneth Robert Smith	1910	July 1932	June 1938	- to Welhome Senior Boys
Bernard S Smith	1912	Sept 1950	Sept 1963	- to Chelmsford
Harold Spicker	1912	July 1950	July 1956	- to Beacon Hill
Kenneth E Tappin		Sep 1963	1964	
W C Towle		Sept 1956	Jul 1963	- Part time
K Turner		Jan 1960		
Kenneth Austin Walker	1923	Sept 1950	July 1964 *	
Roger Warburton	1909	May 1932	March 1935	- Died
Lionel Watson	1905	Sept 1929 *	Sept 1931	
Alwyn H Wardley		May 1949	July 1953	- to Lincoln
L Watson		Sept 1929 *	Sep 1931	
J W Whitworth		Sept 1948	Oct 1948	
Kenneth T Wignall	1923	May 1952	Dec 1953	- from Welholme
B C Wilkinson		Oct 1949		- from St Johns Primary Boys
Derek Wilkinson		Nov 1952	July 1956	
Alec Harman Withers	1898	Sept 1929 *	July 1964 *	- from Harold St Jnr. Boys
J Wheeler		Part time 1956	Aug 1958	
M Woods	1935	Sept 1957	Apl 1961	

* designates either the first or the last day of Armstrong St School

Female teachers

NAME	BORN	START DATE	FINISH DATE	NOTES
Miss Lonerghan		Aug 1944	April 1946	- from Strand St. School - to Nunsthorpe
Mrs Eleanor Nowell		Jun 1941	March 1946	- to Welholme Jun Girls
Mrs Dixon		July 1940	Nov 1945	- to Armstrong St. Girls
Miss Gwenda . C Allen		Aug 1943	Dec 1943	- to Armstrong St. Girls
Mrs Radge		Jun 1943	Nov 1945	- to Nunsthorpe infants
Mrs May A Wright		Jun 1941	June 1942	
Mrs M Woodhall		July 1942	April 1944	
Lillian A Pickering		Sep 1963	1964	

9: PUPIL MEMOIRES

This chapter reveals the rich embroidery of pupil recollections of schooldays and the impression teachers had on their future, making interesting, and at times, amusing reading as they recall long forgotten memories

During the reign of the school from 1929 to 1964 there have been a large number of outstanding teachers who never sought the limelight but diligently taught the boys to a very high standard, and although they may not be mentioned below, this does not detract from the respect they gained from the boys and they are spoken of with affection: Mr Abe, Mr Bristow, Mr Chadwick, Mr Dixon, Mr Fox, Mr Holah, Mr Holley, Mr Hollingsworth, Mr Holmes, Mr Hopkinson, Mr Hotchkin, Mr Kay, Mr Kew, Mr Leake, Mr Leafe, Mr Lee, Mr Marlborough, Mr Merry, Mr Nowell, Mr Potts, Mr Potter, Mr Smith, Mr Spicker, Mr Towle, Mr Withers.

School Life

The school lesson times were 9.00 to 4.00pm with a hour and a half dinner break.

On Fridays, schools in Grimsby & Cleethorpes started at 8.45am and finished at 1.30pm with a break at 11.00 until 11.30. The reason for schools finishing early on a Friday was to allow mothers to pick up their children to enable them to go down dock to pick up their husband's wages. Each week there was great competition to get to the respective trawler owner's office first, as the queues would be gigantic. This weekly ritual became known as the Fish Dock Races. This practice ceased after the War.

The children walked to school, there being no alternative then, regardless of the weather, on average one mile each way, four times a day, five days a week. Short cuts were found via a network of passages and alleyways.

George Moore 1935-1939

Recalls Mr Fuller had the top class and Mr Potts, P T Teacher, took the class swimming to Orwell St. Baths every Monday morning, leaving at 9.00 to walk to the Baths.

In the playground besides football or cricket, a popular game was called SHINTY.

Jim Stewart 1930-1936

I recall being transferred to Armstrong from South Parade shortly after its opening. The new school was meant to be the pride of the town's Education Committee, but the problems began even as it was being built. The marshy nature of the land meant that it was almost impossible to construct firm foundations and as soon as the roof went on, cracks started to appear.

The first day we moved in the walls were being shored up. The bottom parts of the walls were faced in glazed brick and sticking plaster was being put over the cracks in these. Despite its constructional problems, Armstrong was a good school although discipline was strict. Each teacher had his own favourite brand of cane. Mr Walker who took us for Science had a chair leg! The teachers were definitely in charge in those days, but when you had 48 boys in a class you had to be. When he left school in 1936 he was presented with a medal for not missing a single day schooling in six years.

Len Brown (1933 -35)

The teachers I recall were:

- Harry Potts - Short fellow with horn rimmed spectacles

- Bristow – Maths. Used to offer 3p bit if you did right sums, if wrong he called you "little Tommy Noddy" and gave you the stick. He was short, 5' 6" high, dark complexion

- R Warburton - Keen sportsman with a wry neck

- J Kew - Middle aged gentleman and a toff who taught Geography

- A Beales -Big fellow a nice and a good teacher

- F Potter - Tall commanding figure with a deep low voice

- A, Withers - recalls a Picture of a bow of a ship in Art Class

I recall paying a penny for a bottle of milk from Netherland Daires and a Police Fund that visited the school once a year and gave out boots to the needy.

Times were hard and at the Greyhound Track at Little Coates people begged for food.

At the Dock gates one boy was constantly begging for food with the Copper on patrol duty shooing him away. One day he had had enough and locked him up in the Police Box. When he let him go he went to his lunch bag and found the boy had eaten his lunch.

Roy Walker 1941-1946

There was eight of us playing football in the playground after dinner when the ball struck a window, smashing it. There was no one around to witness it and after discussing between ourselves the best cause of action, we decided to go to Mr Horn's room and confess. Mr Horn praised our honesty and courage at coming to him and then gave us all six of the best with his cane!

John Ellerby 1942-45

I recall Mr Lee being an Officer in the Home Guard and one day came to school in his military uniform and demonstrated the operation of a rocket launcher in the school playground. After loading the machine with a dummy solid rubber round he shot the gun at a target on the wall, the shell struck the wall and rebounded back in their direction scattering the boys to cover.

Mr Ricketts took us for Maths and made my life hell - he had a 1" diameter black rod from fixing carpet which he used as cane.

John Chapman 1949- 54

On my first day at Armstrong I was told to get in a row of boys in equal lines in the playground before sorted and taken to your respective class. One of the teachers told me to go to class 1 where a few other boys were waiting. Shortly after the Headmaster came and told us he didn't want to hear any excuses and gave each boy the cane including myself and told us to go back to our designated classes upon which I told him I had been told to come here as my designated class!

Arthur Taylor 1939-41

Recalls a football Shield made in Woodwork class with a clenched fist and forearm for a football trophy.

In the war until they built the shelters they were taught at houses with approximately 5/6 pupils. I recall homework was handed out once a fortnight at Albert Lennon's shed, corner of Gilbey Rd/ Dunmow St corner.

Mr Bristow used to lift his cane ready to strike the offenders hand and then ask him "Do you need it?" The boy would reply "No Sir". Well sit down came Mr Bristow's reply.

Mr Max Holmes had a Sports Shop on the corner of Victoria St. & Riverhead.

Bob Read 1948-52

His parents lived in NewHaven Terrace where he set off to school to walk or from his granny's house in Ayscough St. He recalls one game when he walked to school. A boy with a piece of chalk would write HOP, 10 yards further it would say SKIP and further distance along JUMP with other commands following.

At school in the playground the teachers would take turns on playground duties. One day Bob was knocked over by boys chasing one another shortly after Mr Dixon had blown the whistle indicating everybody to stay still. He took Bob and six other boys involved and caned them on each hand.

He recalls going on a trip to Paris with Mr Withers in charge of 24 boys in 1948/49. They stayed at the Hotel Baucheret in "Filles du Calvert" for bed and breakfast but had an arrangement with a restaurant/café around the corner for meals. Despite the country's reputation for drinking wine even among the youths, Mr Withers instructed the staff to serve lemonade only. He recalls visits to the Sacré Coeur, Notre Dame, Palace of Versailles and Paris Zoo.

I recall that football was played on the Boulevard and we had to walk to any school games. We sometimes used the Public Baths near to the Hospital Nurses' Home to get scrubbed after football.

Bernard Wilkinson 1937-42

Mr Lee took us for Geography and came on an old motorbike

Mr Bristow —Maths and also did a lot of Shakespeare and was nicknamed Brisarno

Mr Horn — Used to read stories from his own personal library. It was fascinating listening to him telling stories and changing his voice for the different characters.

In 1940 the Assembly Hall was banned from use.

George Alltoft 1936- 1941

I was again picked to represent the school at football and in one particular game against Holme Hill on Dec 14th 1937 I scored all seven goals which was reported in the school magazine. I walked to school and the class sizes were approx 45 pupils. We went weekly to Orwell St. Baths for swimming and at woodwork made stools, fire guard (which I still possess), etc.

On the exercise books we used to have times tables on them and also weights and measure tables.

As soon as War was declared the government stopped any public gatherings in the town so Grimsby Town F C played their games at Scunthorpe.

The day before War was declared a large majority of the school children were evacuated to Skegness (2nd Sept 1939), me included. The remaining pupils were organised to be taught in houses. I recall Mr Max Holmes our teacher, who was an all round sportsman and a Grimsby Town player, walking in the sea in his football boots and he told us it was the best thing to bed them in. During the war I also made blackout blinds for our house at Lord St.

Mr Bristow used to teach us chess and would compete against each pupil as he walked around the class and also held competitions at night.

Mr Abe was in charge of the football teams and later Mr Armstrong.

We had Gym every day and we would go into the hall to set up the mats, horses and equipment with Mr Dixon and Mr Nowell, the coaches.

Mr Johnstone took us for Art and in one examination he scrapped all the papers stating they had no light and shade.

I recall one day a boy came into class with a message for the teacher, Mr Withers. His trousers were thread bare and after he'd gone Mr Withers had a collection organised from the class to get him some clothes. We also wanted a football strip so everyone collected bottles and paper to take back for funds towards a new strip.

The teachers were strict discipliners and it was not unusual to have mallets, chalk brushes etc thrown at you.

Norman Vivins 1954-58

Norman lived in Lancaster Ave and went to Armstrong in Sept 1954 going into 1B class with Max Holmes as Form Master and John Holmes, the Headmaster. In 1956 he had progressed to 3A class with Bill Hollingsworth his Form Master and Alf Lee had been promoted to Headmaster.

Norman soon established himself in the football team and due to his height was a successful centre back and an all round sportsman, playing for the 1st Cricket Eleven team. He recalls that on match day they were allowed to leave 20 minutes early to get themselves down to the venue but still had to ask the Teacher of the particular class for permission to leave which was often given grudgingly. Although Norman was tall he recalls that at 14 years of age they still wore short trousers at school. He was also a Prefect at school.

I recall the last class in the corridor before the girls' department was Mr Graham Holley's class, which had severe cracks between the dividing walls due to the building structure suffering from subsidence. Mr Holley confirms that a slope in the corridor leading to his classroom due to subsidence in the floor caused both boys and staff to slide the last few yards to reach his room. More than once the door would jam overnight due to movement. Mr Holley recalls shaking hands with another teacher through a crack in the wall caused by the subsidence.

Dave Blanchard 1947-51

I attended Armstrong St School from 1947 until 1951 and recall the following teachers there.

- Mr Max Holmes was my first Form Master 1947-48
- Mr Leake was my 2nd Form Master 1948-1949
- Mr Dixon was my Form Master for 3rd and 4th year 1949-1951
- Mr Fuller - Art - Used to spit in paint tubs to moisten paint.
- Mr Nowell - Science
- Mr Fox - History
- Mr Withers - Art & French and shorthand
- Mr Dixon - Gardening, Maths & English
- Mr Holmes - Sport
- Mr Forde - Sport, Boxing & Rugby
- Mr Merchant - Maths, Football Team Coach
- Mr Hotchkin - Technical Drawing
- Mr Hollingsworth

George Procter 1947 - 1950

I recall Max Holmes as probably the best all round sportsman the area has produced, although born in South Lincolnshire. He excelled in football, cricket, tennis, hockey, squash, all played at County level.

Harry Abe along with Max Holmes played cricket for Grimsby Town. The team was largely comprised of teachers and fish merchants. I spent many happy hours at Littlefield Lane watching them.

The Armstrong Football team ruled soccer at that time and provided five boys in the Grimsby Boys team.

George Dixon "The enforcer", always took Class 1C, start as you mean to go on! He also took classes to the allotment for gardening.

*Grimsby Town opening batsmen -
Harry Abe and Ben Webster*

Ron Greenacre 1959- 1963

I arrived at school, aged 12, complete with new uniform with a blazer and woven badge with the dock tower proudly enblazed upon it. I was assigned to class 1A.

We had our first Maths lesson, with the legendery Mr Dixon, a giant of a man with an imposing personality, larger than life character, whose enthusiasm affected me greatly in my formative years. There was no doubt who was in charge in his Maths lessons. He went around the whole class asking us who we were, and giving us nicknames. He also took us for road safety lessons, training to get our cycling proficiency badge. After learning to ride our bikes around obstacles in the playground and learning to use hand signals, we were all tested by a police sergeant who came to the school and observed us riding around Armstrong St.

There was an Inter Schools Road Safety Cycling Competition with all Grimsby Schools participating. We showed up at the Police Station, and rode around a course at one minute intervals. There were members of the Cyclist Tourist Club marking us on how we rode our bikes correctly at different points around the course. Armstrong team won. Dicko was given an oilskin cape to present to me as a first prize. In class he asked me why I didn't look very happy. I said I wasn't feeling happy. He replied this will make you smile, he then produced the new cape from his cupboard, and told me I had won the compettion, that sure made me smile and all the class laughed.

Mr Lee generally took assembly every morning with Mr Abe playing the piano for the hymns. Only half of the Assembly Hall could be used, the other half sectioned off and propped up due to subsidence. We would often sing the Hymn "Oh hear us when we cry to thee for those in peril on the sea". We would adulterate the words and sing "Oh hear us when we cry to thee for those in peril in room 3" (Dickos room).

For the 4th and 5th years, the staff organised the annual school dance at the Winter Gardens in Cleethorpe. Prior to the event, weekly dancing lessons were held in the Girls' Assembly Hall, where the boys and girls stood on opposing sides to each other. The boys were told to choose a girl, and ask her to dance. It was a long walk across the Hall, with all my pals watching. What if she said "No thanks", and I had to ask another one? Apparently the girls were more concerned that they might be the last one to be asked. We spent several weeks learning the waltz, quickstep and cha-cha. After each session we were allowed to play pop music and dance with the girls, some of the girls being very good dancers, and I learnt the twist too. A few days before the school dance, we had a dancing lesson from the great Jimmy Stevenson. He had a dance formation team from Grimsby that had appeared and won a television Dance Tournament, called "Victor Sylvestor Come Dancing", Jimmy Stevenson and his wife, Gertrude, having won the prestigeous Carl Allen Award in 1961. The school dance went well with many of the teachers and Govenors attending. Doing the conga holding onto the Girls' Music Teacher in front of me was quite an experience for a 15 year old. A bus was laid on, and we all got home after a great evening.

During the big freeze of 1963 with 6 weeks of continuous snow and frozen ice, the school remained open with pupils and teachers walking or biking to school without fail every day. During this big freeze, the River Freshney froze over for weeks, several inches thick, and we would play and skate on the ice on our way home from school. Dicko told all his classes, and it was repeated in Assembly that we must not skate or go on the ice or we would be in trouble. So, there we were, the same day, thirty kids sliding on the frozen river on the way home from school. Suddenly I saw Mr Dixon's car approach the bridge at Boulevard Ave. It was an Austin 55, registration LEE 535. My pal shouted "Dickos coming", as he got out of his car and stood on the bridge for a long time, identifying individuals. As it was ice, none of us could get to run, and almost all of the kids falling over in blind panic, like rats in a trap, unable to to escape, it was a comical scene. Fortunately, I was on the edge of the ice, and made my escape hastily down a side street. Next morning in class, he asked, stick in hand, for everyone skating on the ice to stand up, telling the class he knew who they were. I stayed seated, my heart pounding, and got away with it. The known culprits were summarily dealt with one by one.

Mr Dixon canoeing on a school camp

Collective Memories of Teachers by pupils

Mr Horn

A well built man, who had served as a Sergeant Major in the First World War, and ran the school like he ran his old battalion. His booming voice could terrorise the whole school. It just vibrated through the building. He came to the school in 1938 as Headmaster transferring from South Parade and remained Headmaster until his retirement in 1948. Mr Horn used to take classes where he would read out stories to the class, taken from his own library. He had a commanding voice and portrayed the characters in the book admirably which would hold a class in total silence as they listened intensely to his voice. A popular short story he told was "The monkey's paw", a gripping yarn that fetched out the best of his talents with his voice impersonations.

Mr Dixon

A No-nonsense teacher whose physical size (ex paratrooper) and mannerisms had every boy in fear (including the hard cases) and you made sure you kept out of his sight. No one messed around in his class but he gained the greatest respect from his pupils. One of his subjects he taught was Technical Drawing and if you made a mistake by substituting a thin line with a thick one you would receive a clip around the ear.

A strict disciplinarian, whose great love, apart from his pipe smoking, was gardening and took a particular pleasure from administering the school allotments down near Cleveland Bridge. He also had his own allotment in Littlefield Lane. This work was allotted to the B and C forms. The A forms took French and saved themselves backache on the allotment.

In one of his Maths lessons he asked the class what an inverted fraction was. Complete silence. He asked if anyone knew what "inverted" meant, silence greeted him as the boys sat their in trepedation with arms folded, scared stiff and frightened to get it wrong. He was not impressed, and to the class amazement, picked up a boy from the front row by turning him upside down and holding him by his ankles, repeated the question. The contents of the boy's pockets, money & pencils fell to the floor. Eventually, one by one, obediently and silently, each boy unfolded his arms and put their hand up to answer. The boy, shaken and red faced, was then put down the right way up, grovelling around on the floor to retrieve his belongings before returning to his seat.

During one hot summer's day, the class was assembled in Room 3 awaiting Mr Dixon to arrive. They were not allowed to talk in class or get up until asking permission. He walked in, the boys all seated as always in complete silence. Mr Dixon decided to open the windows, using a very long pole with a hook attached at the end, as it was a bit stuffy with forty 12 year olds who were adverse to bathing. After opening the windows he stood there, and to the boys' horror, witnessed a boy talking to the boy next to him, oblivious to Dicko glaring at him and getting very angry in silence but with the window opener at the ready. What next? Dicko, a trained ex Paratrooper, adopted a stance as if to do a bayonet charge with a ten foot pole in hand, pointing towards Jones, who was still talking and completely unaware of his pending doom. With that, Dicko let out a blood curdling scream and charged full tilt down the aisle, with his improvised lance. Jones, suddenly made aware and sensing the danger, as the hair on the back of his head stood up, eyes bulging, lifted up his desk lid, his hands shaking uncontrollably, as all his books fell to the floor. Dicko pushed his lance agaist the desk lid as Jones hid behind it, pushing it up and away from him, the desk lid shaking violently. Jones, ashen faced, slowly put down the desk lid, and Dicko pinned him to the back of his chair, the window opener poking in his chest, towering over him with it. Dicko, then growled "Don't talk in class", walked away and carried on with the Maths lesson, as if nothing had happened. The class were still

Mr Abe and Mr DIxon relaxing in the staff room

terrified, thinking that one of their members was going to meet his maker that day!

One day at the end of school time, our class was assembled in the corridor in darkness, when the lads started singing the American soldiers training song "Sound off". Despite Mr Gregory asking for silence, it continued until Mr Gregory caned the whole of the class. A few days later the class was throwing things at each other when Mr Leake arrived. He promptly caned everyone in the class. When our form teacher, Mr Dixon heard about these incidents he threatened everybody that if it happened again he would also cane us all as well. This had a sobering effect on us all.

During one of the inter football games competing in the Horn Cup, in which a pupil was playing, the match ended up 2-2, being refereed by Mr Forde. The pupil remarked in the dressing room that the opposition's last goal was at least 4 yards offside. With that a voice boomed telling him to stay behind after class. The pupil's next class was gardening with Mr Dixon and he knew he would be in trouble if he did not make the lesson on time. His own class had set off to walk to the allotments in Macaulay St. when Mr Forde chastised him before sending him on his way. He ran like the clappers to catch the class up and finally made it as they crossed over the bridge to the allotments in Haven Terrace.

Mr Dixon used to get the pupils to sell off the grown vegetables in order to purchase seeds and gardening utensils. And woe betides you if you were caught opening peas in their pod or eating the produce.

One of Mr Dixon's projects I recall was drawing a map of Grimsby to a large size and putting the street names on it.

Mr Dixon had a 3ft basket cane for discipline and would say "Make my day. The cane was so flexible it could bend like a letter O" and was named "Sleeping Beauty". He would crack it down hard on a desk to wake up the day dreamers.

One pupil recalls brambling at Irby Hill late one Sunday evening and ran across the road in front of Mr Dixon's black A40 car. Oh s..t! he thought as he hit the brakes, his wife lurching forward on the windscreen as the pupil successfully reached the opposite side. The following morning, after a sleepless night, his name was called out in Assembly to report to Mr Dixon's room immediately where he suffered two strokes of the cane and 500 lines stating, Look Right, Look Left, Look Right again and walk across if its safe to do so.

I recall one day at home and there was a knock at the door, when I answered it there stood Dicko as he was nicknamed. I stood their petrified until he explained he had come to pay his bill he owed to my Dad for painting his house.

John (Nobby) Armstrong Woodwork Teacher

He arrived each day to school on his bicycle and often had long lengths of timber tied with string to his crossbar, often assisted by Harry Goulding.

If you walked into his room without knocking a piece of 4" x 4" timber would be thrown at you, and his aim was excellent, and he informed you that you should knock before entering. After being ordered out and told to knock on the door, which you then proceeded to do, he would ignore you despite your repeated knocking.

His method of teaching was to ask the boys to gather around the bench whilst he demonstrated a particular skill. One day after such an instruction, as the boys were gathered around the bench, one lad, Dave Quickfall let off wind which made the boys laugh. Nobby quickly dragged the boy by the scruff of the neck into the stockroom and minutes later he emerged with thick rope laced and tied tightly around his trouser bottoms with Nobby announcing to him and the class "See if you can pass wind now".

John Armstrong, known as Nobby, was also a character. He taught us Woodwork but had his own standard of teaching. A boy would take a stool he was making to show him and he sarcastically would say "you like this do you?" and if it wasn't up to his standard, he would then smash it to bits with a mallet and say start again. If you were threatened of being given the cane, he would on occasions send you in the storeroom where all the wood was kept and let you choose your own weapon (the cane he would use on you). He disliked boys who smoked and regularly you had to line up in a row with your hands extended in front of you to show him your hands for signs of nicotine staining. If you had it was automatic caning. He used to bike to school on a big sit-up-and-beg bike and he always had a canvas carry bag. When the coalmen had been to fill up the coalbunkers in the playground, he used to get a couple of boys to pick up the spilt coal around the bunkers and fill his canvas bag with it. He was a good teacher and was given respect by the pupils. At football he played in the staff team against the boys and he was a rock solid centre half who left his mark on any opposing player. He played for Old Winghams in the Grimsby Football League as a centre half. Later on in life our paths crossed again when I found him to be Chairman of the local Football League and we became good friends.

Mr Goulding (Gogo)

Mr Goulding was a brilliant mathematician and well respected by academic pupils and night school students who were taught by him, but his dry sense of humour made him the most eccentric of characters remembered by the pupils

He always pronounced the letter S as Sh. A typical greeting would be 'You're a shmoker, I can't afford to shmoke, so I shmoke the school chalk" as he prowled around the class with a stick of chalk from the side of his mouth. It seemed odd that his room was number Sheven. Morning Maths lessons always began with a quick fire mental arithmatic going around the class. Get it wrong and you were out of your seat to the front of the class, the walk of shame. However he did give you a chance to "shave your bacon", get the question right and you went back to your desk, if you failed, it was bend over the end of his desk and get a whack from his piece of moganny (mahogany). His method of teaching tables was to chant them and if you were asked the time by him your answer had to be 5 to 8 and then he would chant 5280 feet in a mile, 5280 feet in a mile etc. His calculation chant for the circumference of a circle was Pi D makes C, this was sung with repeats to the tune of Pompey Chimes.

A boy in Norman Vivins class, Kenny Margraves, although small was a heavy smoker which Gogo was aware of. One day he said to Kenny in class "Do you want a fag kid?", to which Kenny replied, yes. He allowed him to light up and whilst Kenny was enjoying the freedom of a smoke Gogo had quietly gone around the back of the class and approached him from the rear. He smacked him around the head and told him "You don't shmoke in my class!"

Gogo was big mates of Nobby Armstrong and when there was an order for teachers to assemble on the quadrangle for a group photograph a pupil was sent from Gogo to Nobby to see if he was going to attend. Nobby would then ask the messenger "was

Gogo going?" So back went the messenger with the message and came back with the reply "I'll go if your going". Needless to say there are very few group photos with Harry Goulding and Nobby Armstrong on.

A pupil recalls his memories of Maths Teacher, Harry Goulding, and a third person – Mr Mahogany. The first time I encountered him was when we entered his room to find him sat on a chair which was perched on top of a desk, holding a piece of chalk and imaginary smoking it. He told us to sit down and then beckoned me: "Come and meet my friend Mahogany". He proffered me this piece of shining wood about 10" long x 2" wide with which I duly shook hands as I went bright red with embarrassment. He then asked me if I wanted a shave or haircut. I didn't know what to say for the best, and therefore replied a shave. He promptly replied that there were no shaves that day so told me to bend over and gave me an almighty slap on the backside with the mahogany.

He named his four blackboards after television manufacturers, BUSH, ECHO, FERGUSON, and FERRANT. He would then ask the class which television screen they would like to choose for the day's lesson.

One day in Mr Goulding's class, a pupil, Lionel Harriman had a mouth organ tucked in his top pocket and Mr Goulding said "Can you play that kid?" and asked him to play, which Lionel did.

Goulding said "I can play one of those. He took the mouth organ from him and then asked for requests and then proceeded to play "Too Young" by Nat King Cole and then carried on with some Frank Sinatra favourites. The whole of the lesson was taken up by his playing and when the bell rang for the end of the lesson the boys had to stand up whilst he played The National Anthem!

I recall being in Mr Goulding's class for an exam. He placed his chair in front of his desk and placed a newspaper on it. He instructed us to open our exam papers and start whilst he would read his newspaper. We thought our luck was in as we could peep over our mate's shoulder but as Mr Goulding sat down and opened his paper it revealed a large 12 inch hole cut through the middle of the paper to allow him to peer through.

One day he asked me to go home, which was nearby, and fetch back two of my mother's best spoons, which I promptly did and returned with the spoons. He then took off the front wheel of his bike, which he used to store in the classroom, and started to remove the tyre from the wheel with the aid of the spoons, telling the class he had got a puncture!

One pupil from an A stream class recalls Mr Goulding taking them to the allotments one hot summer's day instead of the lesson on Religious Instruction. They were detailed to pick raspberries, and when the task was completed, were asked to line up in a row and to have their tongues sticking out to see if anyone had been eating the raspberries. One culprit (red tongued) was promptly caned.

Mr Goulding was my Maths teacher although he taught other subjects too. He used to keep all the ink nib pens in a box on his table and on his command you all rushed to obtain hopefully a decent pen to write with. Irrespective of its condition you were expected to write neatly in ink with it. Some nibs were bent up and twisted but you were expected to write with it or you were punished. Being left-handed had its own problems with writing in ink. Once you had written on the left hand page and continued to write on the top of the right hand page, you had a tendency to smear your previous written work as your arm moved over to the right hand side page. Left handed people seemed to develop a method to overcome this problem; my own method was to write with my wrist twisted in a crook shape holding the pen whilst my left arm circled around the left hand page newly written on.

This pupil also recalls his unique method of punishing was a piece of mahogany which

he gave you the option of stating the form of punishment a, shave or haircut (whacked on the backside or hand). Sometimes after you had stated, your choice he would do the opposite saying "you ain't in my class to be choosy." One pupil when pulled out in class for punishment was asked "shave or haircut?" and after his choice was given, Mr Goulding replied "It's Thursday, half day closing, barber's closed, you're not allowed". He then received both for being cheeky.

Mr Withers

On our first French lesson we encountered Mr Withers who sported a french beret, smoked a pipe, and was very much into the french way of life. His classroom was a prefab outbuilding. He told us how he spent his summer holidays in Provence, and ate frogs and snails which drew grimaces from us all. He played some linguaphone records to help us learn the basics and pronunciation. When we found out 'oui' meant yes, which sounded like wee to 12 year olds mentality, and coq meant chicken, there was much hilarity and giggling and we were threatened with the cane. What a strange race the French seemed to be to us.

Mr Wither's used to fetch loads of apples from his garden to sell at 1p-2p-3p for funds for the Poppy Fund. Mr Withers took art/French and also shorthand. Later in life you would see him playing as a regular at Dominoes at the Ship Hotel.

Mr Withers' class 1937

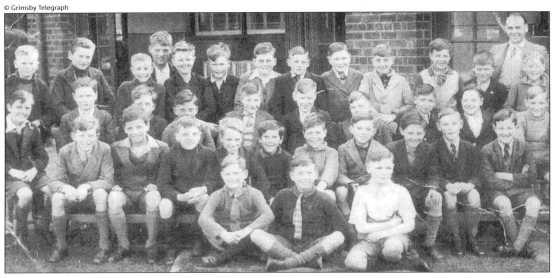

Mr Dingley's class 1939

Mr Abe's class 1938

Mr Nowell's class 1950

Mr Gouldings class 1952

Mike Ramskill, Brian Turner, Les Aitken, Ken Griffiths, Ray Blakey, Ted Loughran, Albert Bradley, Terry Markham

Terry Reeves, Malcolm Gallyer, Pete Glover, Geoffrey Thompson, Ted Day, Skimmer Roberts, Malcolm Hall, Frank Mallinson, Bernard Pearce

Colin Snelson, Brian Elford, Henry Smith, Jeff Elliot, Brian Rhodes, Mr. Harry Goulding (teacher), John Roe, Dave Fletcher, Brian Newton, Bill Marris, Joe Jackson

Mr. Dixons class 1952

John May, Tony Granville, Frank Revell, George Smalley, George Smith, Charlie Woods,

Len Carr, Vic Robinson, Roy Plumtree, Edward Walton, Gibson, Brian Bridges, Pete Waters, Brian Blackett

Harold Jackson, Billy Smith, Carl Waumsley, David Dent, Reg Dixon (teacher), Brian Edwards, Jim Leeman, Mick Mawer, Jack Kennedy

D Brett, D Warman,
C Smith, R Harrison,
Smith, Doy, P Sampson

John Smith, C Marshall,
Lingard, C Needham,
Mr A Lee, K Wright,
– ? –, P Walsham,
W Hewson

Armstrong St School 1952

Mr Hopkinson's class 1954

Mr Leafe's and Mrs Dixon's class 3b1   1945

P Ramsden, N Smith, J Osbourne, E Calvert, R Drayden

M Anderson, M Shepherd, D Rushby, B Richardson, Mr Lee (headmaster), G Howe, E Benson, R Lightfoot, – ? –

Prefects 1956

Roy Leonard, Garry Smith, B Roberts, J Hagor, Geoff Lindley, – ? –, D Smith

Bernard Hogget, J Davis, Pete Claydon (Head Prefect), Mr Lee (Headmaster) Terry Cardy, M Jackson, E Jiles

Prefects 1958

Brian Redding, Michael Sheppardson, David Pearce, Trevor Bird

Graham Parrot, Mike Reece, David Troop, Donald Swindell, Tony Strugnell, Michael Selby, David Garland, John Meggett

Dave Atkin, Martin Watson, Keith Templeman, Reg Dixon (Headmaster), Alan Broddle, Harold Dolby, Derek Barker

Prefects 1963-4

10: SPORTS GALLERY

Armstrong St School had a strong tradition of competing in many sports, against other local schools, at one time holding the cups for football, cricket, athletics and swimming simultaneously. The teams shown here are those who were fortunate enough to be photographed at the time.

Football

1944 Football Team
K Rowley, K Taylor, P Pullan, L Redding, K Roberts, Bratley, Mr Kay (Teacher)
G Osborne (ball), Johnston (cup)
H Leak, B Neal, L Holmes, P Wills

1944-1945 Asher Cup Winner
Roy Walker, Bernard Borman, George Groves
Ted Maddison, Lew Jackson, Eric Wilcox
Ray Cammack , Roy Joass, Sandy Finney, Dennis Smith, George Beecham

1946 Football Team
Max Holmes (Teacher), R Hilton, B Johnson, L Jackson
R Bride, R Joass, D Smith, R Riggall, L Warner
W Lord, M Bielby, B Rigall

1947-48 Football Team

D Seddon, R Bride, L Jackson, H Elsom,
King, R Riggall, Max Holmes (Teacher)

E Reynolds, W Lord, D Hill, D Griffiths, B Riggall

1948-49 Football Team

Max Holmes (Teacher), B Hallett, R Smith,
D Kavanagh, B Hewitt, Gallagher, R Riggall

R Harpen, W Lord, B Riggall, B Holmes, B Parker

1956-57 First Eleven

Kenny Margrave, Fred Nuttall,
Dave Rushby, R Lightfoot

Mr Holley (Sports Master), Mike
Foster, I Draycott, B Patchett, Norman
Smith, Bill Benson, E Briggs, Ray
Gooch, Mr Lee (Headmaster)

1956-57 Football 'A' Team

Clive Genney, John Cook, George
Batty, Malcom Cook

Mr Chadwick (Sports Teacher), Norman
Vivins, Arthur Baxter, Ray Evison, Tony
Inson, Byron Hyldon, Trevor Blythin,
Mike Lee, Mr Lee (Headmaster)

1956-57 Football 'B' Team

J Seddon, B Clarke, J Brocklesby,
R Asher, N Asher, J Smith

Mr H Goulding (Teacher), M Shaw,
C Stevens, B Hoggett, A Austwick,
R Swain, Mr Lee (Headmaster)

1957-58 First Eleven

Mr Lee (Headmaster), Carl Stephens,
Rob Sharman, Mike Lee, Jimmy Grayson,
John Cook, Norman Vivins, Buddy
Roberts, Mr. Holley (Sports Teacher)

Bernard Hoggett, Byron Hyldon,
Arthur Baxter, Ray Gooch, Nobby
Clarke, Mike Jennings, Mike Lynn

1957-58 Football 'B' Team

Les Allan, Barry Arnold, Steve Hoyles, Corny
Snell, John Hyldon, Max Holmes (Teacher)

Steve Carter, Alan Jackson, Donny Davis,
A Clark, George Robinson, B Sylvester, Ray Hall

1958-59 Football 'B' Team

George Dutton, Hodson, Steve Carter, Corny
Snell, Steve Hoyles, A Clark, G Robinson

Mr Reed (Teacher), Ginger Robinson,
Donny Davis, John Hyldon, Ray Hall,
Brian Wallwork, M Woods (Teacher)

1959-60 First Eleven

Les Driver (Teacher), John Robinson, Ronnie Smith, Angus Davison, Barry Rusling, Tony Deans, Mr Lee (Headmaster)

Tony Cooper, Kenny Hodges, Ray Hall, Dave Beecham, Gily Roberts, Mick Chew, Les Walmsley

1959-60 Football 'A' Team

Mr Chadwick (Teacher) , Peter Robinson, Steve Hoyles, John Hyldon, George Robinson, Mr Lee (Headmaster)

Don Davis, Armond Clarke, John Parkinson, Mick Hodson, Steve Carter, Corny Snell, Ray Hall

1959-60 Football 'B' Team

K Hallet, D Woods, G Hodson, G Holley (Teacher), D Preston, D Young, R Bunn

P Unsworth, P Avison, A Burkill, S Taylor, R Stockley, P Deans, T Wallwork

1959-1960 Football 'C' Team

Mr M Holmes (Teacher) Ian Mckenzie, Michael Sheppardson, Dave Robinson, Pete Walsham, Colin Last, Mr A Lee (Headmaster)

Alan Cooper, Dave Garland, Neil Sutton, Michael Wilkinson, Barry Pearce, Robin Edham, Michael Reece

1960-61 First Eleven

Dave Preston, Derek Young, Les Driver (Teacher) Ray Hodson, Steve Carter

Don Davis, Stuart Taylor, Ray Hall, Corny Snell (Capt), John Hyldon, Armond Clarke, Steve Hoyles

1960-61 Football 'A' Team

Dave Garland, Pete Walsham, Neil Sutton, Mr Trevor Chadwick (Teacher), Michael Sheppardson, Robin Edham, Dave Robinson

Harry Dolby, Alan Cooper, Barry Pearce, Michael Wilkinson, Colin Last, Ian Mckenzie, Michael Reece

1961-62 First Eleven

G Holley (Teacher), B Stockley, P Deans, R. Coppock, B. Wynne, P Walsham

B Raper, P Avison, R Bunn, D Preston, D Young, D Garland, K Hallett

1961-62 Under 14s

Robin Edham, Neil Sutton, David Robinson, David Garland, Peter Walsham, Mr Graham Holley (Teacher)

Harold Dolby, Michael Reece, Barry Pearce, Michael Wilkinson, David Pearce, Colin Last, Alan Cooper

1962- 1963 Football 'B' Team

J Bickley, T Robinson , C Shillito, – ? –, B Dillon
– ? – (Teacher), M Nurse, R Turner, G. Hyams, D Nangle, D Robinson, T Ringuth

© Grimsby Telegraph

1963 First Eleven

Ray Gooch, Wilf Stratham, Dave Holt, Nigel Bown, – ? –, Keith Rothwell,

Charlie Blanch, John Sanderson, Paul Schubert, Geoff Burnett, Dave Nangle

© Grimsby Telegraph

1948-49 Staff vs Boys Football Teams

Despite losing 5-6, the school side, one of the best in the area, and the current League champions, certainly wasn't disgraced since the teachers included Danny Dearden (Sheffield United) and Max Holmes (Grimsby Town). Three of the boys (Walter Lord, 3rd from left, and the Riggall twins, fourth left and second right) went on to greater things, all joining Grimsby Town.

1948-49 Staff Football Team

Harry Goulding, – ? –, Nobby Armstrong, Alf Lee, Harry Abe, Bill Hollingsworth, Alec Leake

Tom Herbert, Danny Dearden, Don Hotchkin, Max Holmes, C Forde

1949-50 Staff vs Boys Football Teams

Staff: H Goulding, A Wardley, D Hotchkin, A Lee, S Marchant, M Holmes, H Abe, W Hollingsworth, C Herbert, J Armstrong, J Gregory

Boys: J Strange, Gallagher, Ramsden, G Howard, R Linford, B Elson, F Thompson, J Atkin, H Redding, – ? –, B Parker

1953-54 Staff vs Boys Football Teams

Staff: Graham Holley, Ken Wignall, Tom Herbert, Harry Abe, John Holmes, John Armstrong, Harry Goulding, Max Holmes, Don Hotchkin, Bill Hollingsworth, Dennis Holah, Leslie Peters

Boys: J Doyle, R Holmes, R Lawrence, T Blythin, K Young, R Dolby, S Walker, W Henson, P Waters, S Gibbs, M Harris

Cricket

1947 Cricket Team

W Lord, Mr Leake, D Fox, R Plaskitt, D Seddon, B Riggall, Nichols (scorer) R Riggall

B Hewitt, G Peck, D Griffiths, L Jackson, B Holmes

1948 Cricket Team

R Riggall, G Howard, R Smith, R Plaskitt, B Riggall, B Holmes, W Lord

B Hewitt, D Seddon, Wright, G Peck, D Griffiths

1952 Cricket Team

Roberts, – ? –, Bradley, J Sizer, A Lidgard, James Woodhouse, Carl Needham, John Roe, Tony Bratley

– ? –, John May, John Smith, Harry Abe (teacher), Lawrence, Sid Cullem, Colin Sparkes

Armstrong Cricket Team 1960

Lynsey Shaw, Stuart Taylor, Dave Preston, Alan Woods, Richard Coppock, Tony Wallwork,

Alan Jackson, Paul Avison, Don Davis, Roger Bunn, Barry Sylvestor, Max Holmes (teacher)

Armstrong Cricket Team 1961

Ray Hall, Barry Sylvestor, Geoff Patchett, Ray Hall, Chris Brown, Stuart Taylor

Geoff Mason, John Hyldon, Dave Beecham, Peter Hart, Corny Snell

Net Practise at Chapman St

Dave Beecham and others look on. Eric Burrell with bat under Max Holmes' tuition

Athletics

1948 School Sports Teams

1950 inter school Athletic Team with Grimsby News Cup and various Sports Teams

1950 Inter- Schools Athletics Team

1961-62 Athletics Team

D Beecham, Robinson, J Parkinson, P Gibbs, R Barton, G Mason, M Irving, G Hodgson, J Waters, – ? –, A Davidson

J Hyldon, M Ellerby, G Rouse, D Clixby, C Riggall , R Bunn, H Hooton, – ? –, A Clarke

T Cook, H Dolby , N Dolby, M Wilkinson, R Edham, D Garland, – ? –

Swimming

**1949 Telegraph Shield and
Maddock Cup Winners**
R Saunders, B Collins, J Strange (captain), K Grundman
J Turrell, K Brocklesby

1950 Telegraph Shield Winners
Ken Brocklesby, John Turrell
Mr Lee (teacher) R Saunders, C Grundy,
John Strange, Barry Collins
– ? – presenting the shield with
Mr J Holmes (Headmaster)

1951 Telegraph Shield Winners
Dave Brittain, Ken Brocklesby, John Turrell,
Colin Grundy, Barry Collins, Mike Fenwick

1952 Telegraph Shield Winners
Mr Lee, Markham, Don Warman,
Bradley, Brocklesby, Bray, Bates

Sports Day Programme

Clee Fields, Thursday, June 3rd 1954 at 2.30pm

Referee

Mr. John Holmes, Headmaster

Judges

High Jump: Mr. W Hollingsworth

Long Jump: Mr. H Abe

Shot And Criket Ball: Mr. G Holley

Track Events: Messrs D Wilkinson,
    D Holah, D Hotchkin, D Walker

Clerk Of The Course

Mr M Holmes

Recorders And Announcers

Messrs R, Fox, A Withers, G Boyson

Starter

Mr. H Goulding

Competitors Stewards

Messrs G R Dixon, H Spicker

Spectators Stewards

Messrs A Lee, J Armstrong, D Nowell,
A Hopkinson, G Marlborough, B Smith

Rules

1. The sports will be run as a House Competition, each House to enter two competitors in each track event, and one in each field event.
2. No competitor may compete in more than one track or field event other than relay races.
3. Points to be awarded:
   - 1st = 4 points
   - 2nd = 3 points
   - 3rd = 2 points
   - 4th = 1 point

Colours

Franklin: Blue

Hereward: Green

Newton: Red

Tennyson: Yellow

		FRANKLIN	HEREWARD	NEWTON	TENNYSON
1	**2.30pm 100 yards**				
	Y1	Harvey	Fixter	Harrison	Brittain
		Davies	Roberts	Coultas	Batty
	Y2	Corringham	Smith	Genney	Marshall
		Cook	Parker	Cator	Foster
	Y3	Smith J	Ellis	Cullum	Payne
		Swift	Smith K	Briggs	Potterton
	Y4	Collinson	Fanthorpe	Smith W	Balmforth
		Watkinson	Jackson	Catley	Hand
2	**2.37pm 150 yards**				
	Y1	Young	Caborne	Briggs	Jagger
		Smith N	Wilkinson	Thomas	Neal
3	**2.42pm 220 yards**				
	Y2	Hinch	Scrimshaw	Sleeth	Bromley
		Willey	Hardy	Naylor	Wynne
	Y3	Walton	Kitching	Swain	Sutton
		Pearce [3D]	Spencer	Mortlock B	Brown
	Y4	Stewart	Sharp	Brown	Goodhand
		Ellis	Chester	Gibney	Chesman
4	**2.30pm High Jump**				
	Y1	Fairfield	Osborne	Coultas	Jagger
	Y2	Cook M	Wheatley	Genney	Hostad
	Y3	Stubbs	Fox	Bovill	Potterton
	Y4	Blissett	Sharp	Smith W	Balmforth
5	**2.30pm Long Jump**				
	Y1	Davies	Wilkinson	Harrison	Brittain
	Y2	Elvin	Parker	Cator	Wilson
	Y3	Walton	Ellis	Swain	Sutton
	Y4	Fountain	Smith W	Bown	Bradshaw
6	**2.55pm 75 yards Hurdles**				
	Y3	Ward	Fawcett	Bovill	Tyrrell
	Y4	Fountain	Everett	Cook	Fitchett
7	**3.00pm Putting the shot**				
	Y4	Ellis	Chester	Gibney	Goodhand
8	**3.05pm Sack and Novelty Races** **Sack Race**				
	Y1	May	Carter	Smith D	Robbins
		Forster	Patchett	Wood D	Limb
	Y2	Dunton	Goodwin	Wheatley	Sadler
		Margraves	Nuttall	Shuter	Kelk
	Y3	Chapman	Coulson	Willett	Loftus
		Wright	Broadley	Hubbard	Page
	Y4	Plant	Smith C	Scruton	Thompson
		Curtis	Clark	Goodfellow	Burrell

	FRANKLIN	HEREWARD	NEWTON	TENNYSON
Wheelbarrow Race				
Y1	Parker	Briggs	Hatfield	Thompson
	Woods	Everett	Norton	Fox
Obstacle Race				
Y2	Dugard	Johnson	Heath	Smith H
	Forrester	King	Wynne	Foxon
Boat Race				
Y3	Thompson	Shepherd	Rusling	Walton
	Redding	Holland	Rogers	Wood A
	Kennington	Marshall	Young	Keyworth
	Woods M	Holmes	Moore C	Lee
Y4	Asher	Hodson	Nicholson	Cooke
	Chesman	Fitchett	Lancaster	Volley
	Ellis	Riggall	Barnard	Wallwork
	Johnson	Whiting	Buffam	Herbert
	Everett	Herron	Coates	Black

9   3.20pm Cricket Ball

	FRANKLIN	HEREWARD	NEWTON	TENNYSON
Y4	Anderson	Cooling	Thorton	Glover

10 3.25pm 440 yards

	FRANKLIN	HEREWARD	NEWTON	TENNYSON
Y2	Elvin	Kelk	Cullum	Gibbins
	Green	Wheatley	Dunton	Brown
Y3	Addison	Steele	Nelson	Street
	Pearce (3C)	Thompson	Mortlock J	Bielby
Y4	Elford	Smith W	Thorton	Butler
	Miller	Campbell	Woods	Ramsden

11 3.30pm 880 yards

	FRANKLIN	HEREWARD	NEWTON	TENNYSON
Y3	Stubbs	Fenwick	Smith T	Parker
	Grimble	Rolley	Lee	Jackson
Y4	Jagger	Grimble	Crisp	Bradshaw
	Fountain	Blanchard	Carter	Hodson

12 3.40pm 4 x 110 yards Relay

	FRANKLIN	HEREWARD	NEWTON	TENNYSON
Y1	Harvey	Caborne	Harrison	Jagger
	Smith	Fixter	Briggs	Brittain
	Young	Roberts	Thomas	Smith D
	Calthorpe	Wilkinson	Coultas	Neal
Y2	Corringham	Smith	Genney	Marshall
	Cook	Parker	Cator	Foster
	Hinch	Scrimshaw	Sleeth	Bromley
	Willey	Hardy	Naylor	Wynne
Y3	Stubbs	Steele	Swain	Sutton
	Walton	Ellis	Cullum	Payne
	Addison	Rolley	Bovill	Street
	Grimble	Bradshaw	Mortlock B	Parker
Y4	Collinson	Fanthorpe	Smith W	Goodhand
	Stewart	Grimble	Bown	Balmforth
	Elford	Campbell	Gibney	Bradshaw
	Jagger	Sharp	Thorton	Butters

Horn Cups Swimming Gala

Orwell Street Baths, Wednesday, March 15th 1950 At 7.00pm

Starter:	Mr A L Lee
Judges:	Messrs M Holmes, C Forde, H Abe
Recorder:	Mr. A Leake
Competitors Stewards:	Messrs R Fox, C H Coleman
Door Stewards:	Messrs A H Withers, S Marchant, A Wardley

In Each Event, 4 Marks For A Win, 3 Marks For Second Place, 2 Marks For Third And 1 Mark For Fourth.
Class With The Highest Total Of Marks Is The Winning Class In Its Year

Admission By Programme: Boys 3d. Adults 6d.

1st Year

1 Team Race, 3 Aside, 2 Lengths Each, Free Style

1A	Heeney	Blythin	Lawrence (Capt)
1B1	Roberts	Robertson	Shreeve (Capt)
1X	Bakes	Quickfall	Riggall (Capt)
1B2	Wright	Young	Harris (Capt)
1C	Cummings	Clayton	Pickett

2 Neat Dive

1A Clark, 1B1 Robertson, 1X Halliday,
1B2 Wright, 1C Bell (Capt)

3 Breast Stroke Race, 2 Lengths

1A Clark, 1B1 Shreeve, 1X Riggall,
1B2 Tuplin, 1C Bell

4 Back Stroke Race, 2 Lengths

1A Lawrence, 1B1 Roberts,
1X Playford, 1B2 Harris, 1C Twell

2nd Year

1 Team Race, 3 Aside, 2 Lengths Each, Free Style

2A	Warman	Smith	Brocklesby (Capt)
2B1	Hargitt	Cartwright	Bray (Capt)
2B2	Reveller	Roberts	Barley Capt)
2C	Johnson	Steele	Sparkes (Capt)

2 Neat Dive

2A Smith, 2B1 Barnes, 2B2 Markham, 2C Johnson

3 Breast Stroke Race, 2 Lengths

2A Lidgard, 2B1 Dixon, 2B2 Reveller, 2C Sanders

4 Back Stroke Race, 2 Lengths (1st Leg Without Arms, 2nd Leg Using Arms)

2A Brocklesby, 2B1 Needham,
2B2 Turner, 2C Sparkes

3rd Year

1 Team Race, 3 Aside, 2 Lengths Each, Free Style

3A	Braham	Turner	Brittain (Capt)
3B1	Fenwick	Hughes	Collins (Capt)
3B2	Brimsden	Walmsley	Tarrell (Capt)
3C	Davidson	Bell	Grundman (Capt)

2 Diving For Objects (1 Dive From Side & 1 Surface Dive)

3A Braham, 3B1 Blendell, 3B2 Page, 3C Broadley

3 Plunge

3A Maxted, 3B1 Blendell,
3B2 Sparkes, 3C Johnson

4 Medley Team Race, 3 Aside, 2 Lengths Each

	Backstroke	Breast Stroke	Crawl
3A	Peers	Turner	Brittain
3B1	Hughes	Spinks	Collins
3B2	Walmsley	Clarke	Tarrell
3C	Bell	Halliday	Grundman

4th Year

1 Team Race, 3 Aside, 2 Lengths Each

4A	Smith	Strange	Redding (Capt)
4B1	Grady	Brett	Atkin (Capt)
4B2	Carlisle	Pullen	Tanner (Capt)
4C	Asher	Brown	Morton (Capt)

2 Life Saving Race

	Rescuer	Patient
4A	Redding	Leak
4B1	Brett	Grady
4B2	Tanner	Wallwork
4C	Asher	Damm

3 Breast Stroke Race, 2 Lengths

4A Saunders, 4B1 Barnes,
4B2 Carlisle, 4C Simmonds

4 Back Stroke Race, 2 Lengths

4A Hill, 4B1 Stiff, 4B2 Hodgson, 4C Damm

11: The Junior School

The school originally opened with a complete junior section, admitting pupils from four contributory schools. The abundant lighting and ventilation was a vast improvement on the overcrowding and squalor of the classrooms previously used.

The junior school was designed to accommodate 320 mixed juniors. In the junior department it contained ten classrooms, an adequate cloakroom and a 30ft square playroom and had its own separate entrance to the school. Each of the youngsters had a tiny chair and desk with folding desks in some of the junior rooms. It was opened on September 1929 and ceased to be a junior school in 1939 after re-organisation due to the 1936 Education Act.

Teaching Staff 1929- 1938

NAME	START	FINISH
*Miss M Atkinson	Oct 1929	May 1932
*Miss E R Bates (Head)	Oct 1929	Aug 1938
*Miss A Blackburn	Oct 1929	June 1931
Miss Marjorie E Burrell	Aug 1937	Aug 1938
Miss Zara Chrispin	Jan 1930	
Miss Audrey V Cook	Sept 1936	Aug 1938
Mrs Cox	May 1938	
Miss Elizabeth Darlow	July 1934	
Miss E Ferne	June 1934	
Miss M Gardham	July 1932	
Mrs Gresham	Mar 1930	Aug 1932
Miss Louisa Hand	June 1935	
*Miss W E London	Oct 1929	Aug 1932
Miss Lucy Mackrill	Aug 1933	
*Miss I R Manners	Oct 1929	Aug 1938
*Miss M Melton	Oct 1929	
Miss C Patterson	April 1930	Aug 1938
Miss Doris Roberts	Sept 1936	Sept 1937
Miss Hilda M Shatford	Feb 1935	
*Miss D Skippings	Oct 1929	
Miss Helen E Steele	July 1932	
*Miss G L Thompson	Oct 1929	Aug 1938
Miss Maud Wareham	June 1935	
*Miss M Whitham	Oct 1929	Aug 1932

* Member of staff at opening

Re-Organisation (1939)

The 1936 Education Act provides for the raising of the school leaving age to fifteen years of age from September 1st 1939, with exception of those children who, not having attained the present school leaving age, obtain employment regarded by the Local Education Authority as beneficial. Under the Act it becomes the statutory duty of the Local Education Authority to provide the necessary additional senior school accommodation

Prior to the passing of this act, the Board of Education issued instructions detailing the administrative measures necessary to implement the reorganisation of schools, to remedy defective premises, and to reduce the size of over-large classes.

The following building programme, if carried out, will enable the reorganisation of schools in Grimsby to be completed and will provide the necessary additional senior school accommodation for the raising of the school leaving age. The objectives of development are:

The replacement of defective buildings.

The provision of full facilities for all departments in accordance with standards laid down on Elementary School Buildings.

Additional accommodation for the seniors of the 14-15 age group who will remain in school after the 1st of September, 1939.

The reduction of over-large classes to a maximum of 50 on roll in infants and junior departments and 40 on roll in senior departments.

The aim of the reorganisation is an

improvement in the facilities and amenities of the schools which, turned to advantage by the teachers, will ensure for each child a wider and fuller development equipping them for a more understanding and useful citizenship.

Armstrong St School is to be altered to satisfy the requirements of a modern senior school for 480 boys and 480 girls. Plans have been approved by the committee and submitted to the Board of Education

(Taken from Education Committee Books)

His Majesty Inspection Report

This new school was opened in September 1929. The Local Education Authority have been generous in equipment and both children and staff may be regarded as fortunate in their surroundings.

The pupils were recruited from four contributory schools, and it has naturally been a difficult task to bring into an homogeneous whole children who had previously been taught by varying methods. Further, during the period under review, over 200 children have entered school for the first time.

The Headmistress has approached her task with courage and insight, and she has been loyally supported by a capable hardworking staff of teachers who are clearly desirous of doing their best for the pupils placed in their charge.

Very satisfactory progress is being made. The children are interested in their lessons, and were by no means unwilling to respond to tests set during the inspection. The teaching of Reading deserves special praise: the children not only read aloud particularly well, but show more than average ability to grasp the subject manner. In other subjects of fundamental importance, the well-directed efforts of the staff are bearing fruit, and the progress, which has already been made, affords ample ground for confidence in the future.

The last pupil admitted into the school junior register was on 14th July 1938 numbered 509, the register starting in 1935. Unfortunately the first mixed register for the school (1929 – 1935) has not been deposited in the local archives and therefore a grand total of juniors admitted to the school cannot be given.

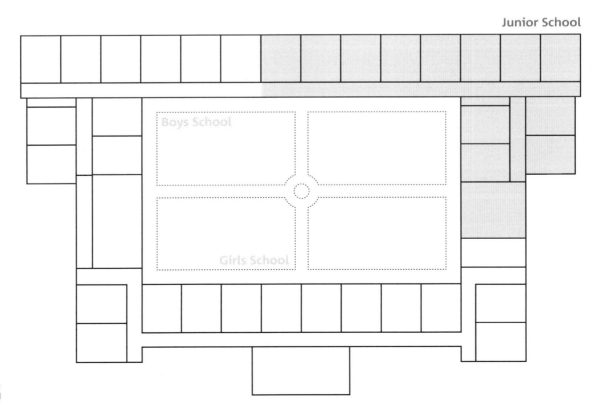

Junior School

12: The Girls' School

The Girls' department opened with 8 classrooms and special sections for cooking, laundry, housewifery and an assembly hall. After the closure of the Junior School in 1938 an additional 5 classrooms and Horsa huts were added.

The school opened in September, 1929 with Miss H Grey as Headmistress and comprised the following staff:

Miss I Gott, Miss I Chapman, Miss G Bright, Miss M Pickwell, Miss K Ryder, Miss P G Lane

The Girls school was a disciplined and well run organisation throughout its reign. The teaching staff were strict but fair and the pupils had respect for them. Miss Hebe Gray would not tolerate truancy and would send a teacher around to the house to get the girl back to school.

H M Inspectors Report

5th December 1930

The school has been open for little more than a year. The time is opportune, however, to pass under review the organisation, and also the aims and ideals by which the Head Mistress has been guided in drawing up the course of instruction.

At the outset it may be stated that the school produces a very favourable impression. In each of the eight classes a good tone prevails; the girls are well mannered, and the staff deserves special commendation for the spirit in which they approach their duties, and for the interest they display in their pupils' welfare.

The Head Mistress has shown sound judgement in dealing with the organisation and the instruction. She has wisely realised that those pupils who are dull and backward need a different kind of treatment from those who are more gifted, and this finds expression in the schemes of work. She has also taken advantage of the academic qualifications of her staff by allowing them to specialise in their respective subjects.

It has admittedly been a difficult task to weave into a corporate whole children admitted from four different schools, at two different dates during the year.

As may be expected there are shortcomings in the attainments of some of the girls, for which neither the Head Teacher nor the staff can be held responsible, and of which they are only too well aware. But on the other hand there is much that is distinctly good. The pupils are interested in their studies; they are being introduced to good literature; they are being trained where possible to find out information for themselves; the written exercises are neatly set out and everywhere the supervision by the staff is most thorough.

Even in the cases of the weaker pupils there is abundant evidence that through the zealous efforts of the staff marked progress is being made.

In short, so much has already been accomplished that confidence in the future is amply justified.

Staffing in 1938

At the beginning of September term 1938 the following staff for the Senior Girls Dept were:

Miss Hebe C Gray (Headmistress), Miss Phyllis G Lane (Deputy Head), Miss Marjorie Ayres, Miss Miriam Pickwell, Miss Sadie Spendiff, Miss Phyllis M D Disney, Miss Rene Dales, Miss Ivy S Clark, Miss Mary Carter-White, Miss Linda D Haswell, Miss Hettie Metcalf, Miss Barbara S Harrison, Miss Audrey Benton and two vacancies.

Report to School Governors

by H Gray (Headmistress) June 1946

The Girls' Department of the Armstrong Secondary Modern School had 534 girls on the Roll at the beginning of the Autumn Term September 1945. Of these, 42 girls (14 +years of age) left in December, and a further 30 at Easter 1946. At the same time 33 girls were transferred from the South Parade Primary School on 10 May 1946, so that the present number of girls on the Roll is 484. There are 15 members of the Staff. This number includes one mistress for Domestic Science.

Organisation

The School is organised into 3 streams. When a girl is admitted to this Department she is tested and classified as A, B, or C, according to her intelligence. She is then placed in her appropriate form, there being 3 or 4 forms A, B, or C, of her particular age group. The child usually remains in the same type of class throughout her school career unless she shows marked improvement.

At the present time there are the following forms:

FORM	AGE	CLASSIFICATION	TOTAL
1st yr	11 yrs	A, B, C, C-	168
2nd yr	12 yrs	A, A-,B, C	182
3rd yr	13 yrs	A, B, B-, C	101
Total			484

For purposes of discipline, self management and competition the school is organised into 4 Houses, each with 2 Prefects and three Mistresses. House marks are given or deducted for work and behaviour and sport.

A House Meeting is held monthly and records are kept of the House marks; the winning House for the year having its name on the School Shield. House Sports for the House Cup are held annually.

Curriculum

The children in the A, A-, B Forms have a greater amount of academic work than the girls in the lower grades who receive additional practical work. All the usual subjects are taken but each subject (except Arithmetic) is taken by a member of the staff who specialises in that particular subject. In addition to the normal academic course a second language, French, was included in the curriculum 3 years ago.

French is now taken by all the girls in the A and A- Forms.

One of the aims of the School has been to try to turn out girls who can take their places in the world and make a worthy contribution as useful citizens. With this end in view the girls are trained to accept responsibility, to undertake any task with cheerfulness, and to have pleasent and easy manners. From the fact that employers continually ask for more of our girls and that His Majesty's Inspector in his last report commented on the poise, bearing and self-reliance of the older girls, I feel that we have in some measure achieved our aim. Good reports have been received of many of the girls who have served in his Majesty's Forces in many parts of Europe.

Suggested Plans for the future

After the 1st April 1947, we shall have to cater for the 14-15 year age group. Of the 182 girls in 2nd year it is interesting to note that of this number 56 only will be eligible by age to leave by the 1st April 1947, so that 126 girls of this age group will remain until they are 15 years of age.

For this Age Group I propose:

- To continue academic work to a higher level with both A and A- streams, including a more advanced course of French.

- To form a Commercial Class for suitable girls, the course to include typing, book-keeping, shorthand.
- To continue aesthetic training in Music, Art and Literature to a higher standard.

For the girls who cannot benefit from any of the above courses I suggest :

- Additional Craft and Needlework
- At least one session per week in Cookery or Housewifery (including Laundry and Mothercraft)

To carry out these plans I shall need additional Staff and equipment.

Staffing

- A well qualified Mistress for English and English Literature.
- A second Music Specialist.
- At least one or possibly two Domestic Science Teachers, (At present only 140 girls can take Cookery or Housewifery weekly on account of accommodation).

Equipment

- An Art room with a stage.
- A Special Needlework Room equipped with wardrobe cupboards, ironing boards, full length mirrors, electric points, large cutting out tables and a wash basin. These girls would then be able to give the whole of one afternoon, or morning, to this subject which is of such vital interest and use to every girl.
- Additional accommodation for Domestic Science.

When conditions make it possible to carry out my schemes I hope to be able to offer to every girl entering the school, the type of education which will give full scope to her natural abilities and talents.

21st Birthday, Sept 1951
Headmistress Miss Gray and Head girl Sheila Hubbard cutting the birthday cake on the schools 21st Birthday with other school prefects and the oldest and youngest pupil present

Staff Changes

A recommendation to the Education Committee that the Specialist posts at the Girls' School in respect of the year 1947-48 be allocated as under:

- First Assistant - Miss P G Lane
- Second Assistant - Miss G E M Shatford
- Third Assistant - Miss M Pickwell

On 15th May 1952 the Education Committee held interviews for 3 candidates for the post of Headmistress:

- Miss C I Bonnello, MA Stamford
- Miss G E M Shatford, BA Grimsby
- Miss M Parkhouse, BA Luton

On the 17th June 1952 they announced the appointment of Headmistress as Miss C I Bonnello.

On 1st Sept 1954 the following appointments were made:

- First Assistant Miss P Disney
- Second Assistant Mrs G Brooks

In Oct 1956 the following staff departmental changes were made:

- Deputy Head - Miss P Disney

- English Dept - F Dulson

- Maths Dept - Mrs G Brooks

- Needlework - Mrs JM Robinss

- Physical Training - Miss EB Harvey

On 30th April 1958 Miss CI Bonnello resigned her post as Headmistress.

Miss P Disney who was Deputy Head was appointed as Acting Headmistress by the Education Committee on 21st April 1958.

G Brooks was appointed as Deputy Head in September that year.

In 1959 Mrs S Pinchbeck was appointed as Head of Mathematics Dept and Mrs W Smith responsible for Needlework.

Building Alterations

The Education Committee decided in 1958 to put out for tender the demolition of the Girls' Assembly Hall. The tender by E & S Smith of 112 pounds was accepted and the work to clear the site and create flower beds was completed by Dec 1959.

School Life

In Feb 1949 it was resolved at a Governors meeting that the proposed school badge and uniform submitted by the Headmistress be approved.

By now the area in general had begun to prosper, and there was a willingness from the girls to adhere to a school uniform. Before then it was only the Grammar school pupils who wore uniforms. It was instilled upon the girls that they wear the school blazer with pride and not do anything that would bring the school into disrepute. This consisted of navy gymslip and white blouse with a tie of diagonal yellow and navy stripes. The school blazer was navy with a lemon piping around the edges of the blazer. The school badge sewn on the breast pocket was a pale blue shield with a diagonal stripe and 3 Prince of Wales feathers as a motif. The netball

Armstrong Girls Prefects and Acting Headmistress 1952
Eleanor Boucher, Sandra Honeyman, Pamela Capps, Norma Miller, Mavis Blackett, Shirley Rands, Beryl Swinburn
Kathryn Stow, Mavis Glover, Valerie Wilson, Miss Lane (Acting Headmistress), Shirley Cardy, Barbara Blain, Nancy Stroud.

teams competing with other schools wore a white blouse, navy blue knickers and a pale blue sash. It was in Sept 1939 that an Education Act was passed for school leaving age to be raised from 14 to 15 years of age. This was started in 1947 which meant additional classrooms were required. This was solved by provided and installing two large Horsa Huts in the girls' playground. One had 2 needlework classrooms and housed Domestic Science whilst the other catered for 2 classrooms and a cloakroom.

The girls were taught a variety of subjects including Verse Speaking and Housewifery. The school had a flat upstairs consisting of a kitchen, lounge, bedroom and bathroom and the girls were instructed in cleaning and polishing the furniture in all the rooms. The students recall being taught to clean a hairbrush by dipping it up and down in a bowl of soapy water to remove the hairs easily. They were taught to wash and iron a duster and clean a handkerchief.

They were taught how to cook meals and make pastry, favourite dishes being brandy snaps, scones and doughnuts! At Christmas time the girls also learned to bake Christmas cake with marzipan covering and icing. Later the Cookery classes were taken in one of the huts in the playground

In Needlework and Sewing, Miss Spendiff would ensure that the first job for all the new intake of girls would be to make their own cookery cap and apron. The apron was a green and white striped material with a white band sewn at the top where the girls embroided their names. They also made a needlework bag with their names on. As they progressed the girls would make themselves frocks which the teacher then expected them to model on parents open day much to their embarrassment! One student recalls making a pram set for her older sister with Miss Spendiff helping her with the delicate sewing.

In the early part of winter, Mr Jimmy Stephenson of Stephenson's Dance School came once a week to teach the boys and girls to dance the Waltz, Square Tango, and other steps. The girls would sit at the back of the hall and the boys were led in and told to select a partner. This was extremely embarrassing for many shy boys and girls as numbers dwindled down and remaining girls hoping they would be selected. At Christmas the boys and girls school combined to hold a Dance at the Winter Gardens for the pupils and teaching staff.

The girls had various educational trips to Stratford upon Avon to the Shakespeare Theatre. The Lake District, camping with Miss Harvey & Miss Ellis and day outings to York, Flamborough Head, Chatsworth, Matlock, and Blue John Caverns and other places of interest. This usually took place early on Saturday mornings with return at night. They were allowed to camp at Humberstone YMCA Camp using the Nissan huts for accommodation. One of the pupils remembers being told to strip off their clothes and being herded into the showers by Mrs Jackie Trueman, despite their protests, trying to cover their bits and pieces with a decorum of modesty.

There were regular drama plays when the girls competed with other schools and they had trips to the newly built Chelmsford School (who had built an amphitheatre in the grounds) to see productions of "A midsummers Dream" and other plays.

On the 2nd April 1957 at the Girls' Speech Day at the Town Hall, the Headmistress, Miss Bonello, noted the increase in the number of students who had decided to continue their full time studies at the Grimsby College of Further Education.

The Mayoress, Mrs. Quinn, presented the prizes to the pupils and was presented with a boquet by Christine Willett.

Armstrong Street Girls Junior & Senior Choir 1951
Cup held by Valerie Wilson

The prize-winners were:

T Rawlings, W Grant, Janet Smith, Joyce Smith, J Cooper, S Moore, A Smith, P Dowse, P Wharton, K Hurst, V Pocken, J Walker, H Harvey, L Smith, S Ball, M Fraser, A Followes, KTeanby, E Burton, A Muir, J Cook, R Colebrook, M Hessey, C Isaac, J Walker, S Austwick, P Summers, J Pearson, M Bygott, C McCrum, J Hyldon, V Green, M Smith, M Flett, M Smith.

The Girls' Choir, which consisted of a Senior and Junior choir, were very successful over the years, winning at music festivals, held on the pier and the Central Hall. Every December there was a Carol concert where choirs from all schools were represented. The Conductor and Music teacher, Miss Shatford, who was a very dedicated teacher, would sometimes have rehearsals at her home. She formed a formidable choir each year of her reign and it was said she could distinguish a bad note from 20 feet away!

Christmas 1961

Ald Pearson & his wife welcome the prefects of Armstrong St. Girls School at the Town Hall

Susan Burkill, Denise Mc Kinley, Glenys Clayton, Marion Simpson

Lorraine Evely, Josie Dalton, Maureen Jones, Carol Ratcliffe

Christine Saunders, Jean Davies, Ald Pearson & Mrs Pearson, Janet Davies, Lesley Mallinson

1948 Class

Pauline M Kenzie, Maureen Fox, Audrey Atkin, June Brown, Edna Hessey, Brenda Miller, Catherine Marshall, Margaret Nicholson, Winifred Draper, Thelma Bradley, Sheila Galyer, Cynthia Page

Susan Codd, Frances Greetham, Marion Brown, Thelma Green, Jean Fox, Sheila Shipp, Pat Doyle, Pamela Capps, Shirley Clark, Eileen Creese

Barbara Newton, Maureen Edge, Louis Johnson, Walters, Rita Homley, Jean Lord, Barbara James, Barbara Boyington, Norma Woods, Maureen Ogelsby, Maureen Bovill

Ivy Pritchard, Mary Frances, Dorothy Wilson, Nancy Stroud, Roma Johnson, Pat Jacklin, Pauline Miller, Margaret Wright, Anita Preston

Class 1A 1949

Valerie Wilson, Marie Gerard, Pat Tuplin, Jean Meadows, Pat Buffam, Maureen Wackett, Marjorie Green, Margaret Shepherd, Barbara Gamble, Shirley Cardy

Ursula Bemrose, Gillian Saunders, Gertie Johnson, Cynthia Adams, Barbara Blain, Ann Carlton, Ann Hardy, Valerie Bedford, Doris – ? – , Marjorie Couldstone

Shirley Colebrook, Elizabeth Blanchard, Mary Strange, Eleanor Boucher, Shirley Rands, Irene Walker, Eileen Potter, Barbara Barron, Vera Chapman, Eileen Tear, Norma Miller

Janet Green, Pauline Scruton, Ann Wilkinson, Vera Brittain, Beryl Swinburn, June Warr, Rosemary Hannah, Eileen Waumsley, Betty Glover

Class 3/4A 1949

Brockelby, – ? – , Mercia Austwick, Barbara Laceby, Coral Page, Terasina Corcoran

– ? – , – ? – , – ? – , Margaret Sullivan, – ? – , Shirley Payne, – ? –

– ? – , Sheila Hubbard, June Sandvig, Ida Gosling, Marjorie Jolly, Jean Brown, – ? –

Margaret Harris, Margaret Garthwaite, Pat Snow, Janet Hawkins, Margaret, – ? – , Pat Withers

1949 Class

Norma Riggall, Shirley Patterson, Marian Davies, Maureen James, Kathleen Anderson, Vera Patrick, Shirley Robinson

Joan Clarke, Dorothy Gardener, Barbara Robinson, Miss Shaw (Teacher), Beryl Cranmer, – ? – , Valerie Walton

Brenda Goddard, Ann Hockney, Megan Robinson, Joyce Riggal, Vera Bromley, Ethel Weston, Freda Everson

1949- 50 Class

Pearl Wright, Beatrice Burnham, Marie Roberts, Irene Johnson, Jane Fitchett, Valerie Hayes, Valerie Lacy, Brenda Bingham, Florence Stroud, Evelyn Burchell, Judith Boyce, Joan Penistone.

Barbara North, Ann Potter, Josephine Dolby, Brenda Lidgard, Cynthia Love, Kathleen Tear, Maureen Smith, Carol Jones, Margaret Dowson, Mary Hoggett, Frances Robinson, Maureen Marshall.

Fulcher twin, Margaret Harvey, Lily Cable, Catherine Walkinton, Doreen Seddon, Sylvia Evison, Patricia Robinson, Maureen Lilly, June ?, Barbara Acklam, Anne Genney,

Marion Constable, Patricia Foot, Marjorie Cotton, Anne Payne, – ? –, Anne Pullen , – ? –, Norma Davies, Fulcher twin, Valerie Whitby, Annette Sharpe

1949-50 Class

1952 Class

1952 Class

Sheila Gayler, Cynthia page, Betty Darnell, Frances Steadman, Pamela Doyle, Shirley Clark, Barbara Newton, Thelma Green, Anita Preston

Mary Boon, Elizabeth Blanchard, Brenda Miller, Catherine Marshall, Dorothy Sanderson, Mavis Blackett, Norma Woods, Sheila Shipp

Margaret Wright, Mavis ?, Ivy Pritchard, Rosie Gale, Pat Jacklin, Ann Hotson, Mary Frances, Nancy Stroud, Maureen Bovill

1952 Class

Marleen Miller, Pat Charlesworth, Merril ? , Sylvia Pearson, Maureen Warner, Diane Warman, Pat Barley, Evelyn Jackson, J George, Janette ?

Doreen Simpson, Sandra Hubbard, Josephine Ray, Valerie ? ,Jean Blackmore, Pam Carrott, Sadie McNore, Janet Evans, Joan Beasley, Sandra Woods, Pat Willey, Carol Green

Beryl Hinch, Valerie Parrish, Shirley Coulson, Jeanette and Jaqueline Jaques , Lily Palmer, Kathleen Herbert, Rose Barton, Emily Russel, Jean Brumfield, Pat Carrott

Class 4A 1952

1955 Class

1960-1961 Class

Joan Renshaw, Rosemary Hill, Jean Arthur, Susan Thurston, Marjorie Nice, Janet Hales, Lorraine Everly, Jennifer Lynn, Barbara French

Susan Appleton, Carol Firth, Josie Dalton, Julie Stimson, Christine Sutton, Joyce Parks, Margaret Chapman, Glenys Clayton, Denise McKinley, Margaret Scott, Pamela Godfrey, Carol Ratcliffe, Mrs J Dixon (Teacher), Margaret Osborne, June Wardle

Diane Bickley, Ann Dunton, Janice Robinson, Jean Davies, Janet Davies, Susan Burkhill, Christine Smith, Lesley Henrickson, Susan Bell Sandra Burrell, Lesley Mallinson

Nativity Play 1950

Trial by Jury

Two scenes from the play" Trial by Jury" presented on July 1956 shows the full cast below who were:

Melanie Nuttall, Pamela Bloy, Margeret Hessey, Christine Isaac, Anita Fellows, Daphne Horsfall, Pamela Hannah,

Pat Haith, Gillian Tock, Keitha Teanby, Evonne Carter, Rosie Topham,

Valerie Dunthorne, Hazel Hodges, Sandra Walton, Maureen Tyson, Mary Isherwood, Ann Barraclough, Annie Muir, Doreen Allan, Hazel Markham, Margaret Scales.

Carol Fenwick, Janice Robinson, Sandra Austwick, Joyce Stevens, Janet Marlow, Marie Robinson, Valerie Green, Ann Robinson, Maureen Handley, Maris Ward, Sandra Snell, Olive Hardy

1952 Sports Team

Sheila Shipp, Anita Haigh, Barbara Newton, – ? –, Maureen Wackett, Betty Snape, Barbara Blain, Thelma Marshall

Eleanor Boucher, – ? –, Marlene Kirk, Dorothy Taylor, – ? –, Shirley Rands, Maureen Mason, Jean Bradley, Helen Thomlinson,

Valerie Newton, Pat Kirk, Yvonne Middlemass, Brenda Hill, Norma Hill, Jeanette Jacques, Jacqueline Jacques, Brenda Bradley, – ? –

1955 Netball Team

Irene Walker Edith Walker

Valerie Harrison, Brenda Hill, Barbara Blain, Norma Hill, Dorothy Jones,

1961-62 Netball Team

Ann Flarty, Janet Snell, Mrs Jackson, Joyce Taylor, Jane Bratley

Sue Carlton, Nina Barton, Maureen Brumpton

1960-61 Netball Team (League Champions)

Carol Carlisle, Sandra Smith, Mrs Jackson, – ? –, Lorraine Everly

Barbara Campbell, Lesley Mallinson, Jane Grey

1958-59 Netball Team

Gail Burns, Carol – ? –, Angela Osborne, Lesley Mallinson, Audrey Deforges, Susan Trafford, Carol Hutchins

1959-1960 Netball Team

Carol ?, Audrey Desforge, Mrs Jackson, Jane Grey, Gail Burns
Angela Osbourne, Lesley Mallinson, Carol Hutchinson

Janet Smith, Jane Bratley, Maureen Brumpton,
Nina Barton, Ann Flarty, Joyce Taylor, Mrs Jackson

1961-62 Netball Team

Joan Arthur, Jane Grey, Lorraine Everly, Rosemary Hill
Janet Davies, Lesley Mallinson, Joan Davies

Inter School Netball winners

Mrs Jackson, Jackie Trueman
Lesley Mallinson, Lorraine Everly, Nina Barton,
Christine Hyldon, Jane Grey, Joan Arthur, Rosemary Hill

Armstrong Senior A Team

Diane Brown, Maria Palmer, Christine
Hyldon, Margaret Yarborough,
Sheila Tyson, − ? −, Maria Platt

Armstrong B team

Barbara Campbell , − ? −, Wendy
Wilkinson, − ? −, − ? −, Linda Simpson,
Lyn Burchell, Carol Carlisle, − ? −

Armstrong Junior Team

Jane Hyldon, Pam Bagshaw, Brenda
Osborne, Margaret Brown, Jean
Charlesworth, Edna Yarborough,
Karen Smith, Jean Thornally

Teaching Staff 1939

H Metcalf, P Lane, M Pickwell
P Disney, I Clark, Miss Findlay,
S Spendiff, Miss Kemp, Miss
B Harrison, A Benton

Miss Mary Carter-White, Miss R
Dales, Miss E Windsor (Cookery
Teacher), Miss Gray (Headmistress)
Miss M Crothers (Cookery Teacher)
Miss L Haswell, Miss M Ayres

PE Teachers are in School Uniform

© Grimsby Telegraph

Teaching Staff 1950

Miss C Watson, Miss P Disney,
Miss D Reynolds, Miss L
Wilkinson, Miss J Shaw, Miss
V Mowat, Miss E Buchanan

Miss J Oak, Miss P Presswood,
Miss P Lane (Deputy) Miss H Gray
(Headmistress) Miss G Shatford,
Mrs. G Brooks (nee Bright),
Mrs M Towriss

Miss R Parrott, Miss J Ellis, Miss
M Forster (Secretary), Miss J
Hammond, Miss M Bridges

(not pictured were Miss E
Harvey and Miss Joan Ellis)

© Grimsby Telegraph

Teaching Staff 1951

Mr Partridge, Mr Jones,
Mr Beveridge, Mr Strickland, Mr Peers

Miss Oak, Miss Fidell, Miss Bridges,
Miss Foster, Miss Parrot, Miss Baxter,
Miss Dennis, Mrs Montgomery

Mrs Dixon, Miss Hammond,
Miss Harvey, Miss Disney,
Miss Lane (Head), Miss Shatford,
Miss Shaw, Miss Watson, Mrs Brook

Memories of a Teacher

Mrs Jean Robins (Nee Oak) 1947 to 1959

I was born in Torrington Street and after leaving school went to teach at Welholme School for approximately 10 weeks before going back to College for Teacher Training.

In 1947 I received a teaching post at Armstrong St. Girls' School where I taught Geography, Biology, Needlework and Maths and English until leaving in January 1959 to teach at Welholme and Pelham.

I recall 16 classes of A to D stream, year 1 to year 4 and 1 class for School Leavers born between September and December.

There were approximately 800 girls on the register with about 250 girls' intake each year

The school had a badge and a motto. There were four House names & colours:

- **Red** – St. Elizabeth
- **Yellow** - St. Joan's
- **Blue** – St. Cecilia's
- **Green** – St. Winifred's

Miss Gray, the Headmistress was a tall, thin and very eloquent woman with long pointed fingers and chestnut coloured hair. She was very strict but well respected by teachers and pupils. She dealt adequately with disputes by standing over the balcony, leading to her study, talking to the complainant, allowing them to move upstairs at her choosing to the next landing. Whereupon by the time they had reached the top of the stairs she had effectively defused the problem with the complainant becoming quite calm and rational.

The school had a logbook and Disciplinary Book where entries of punishment had to be recorded. It was testimony to Miss Gray that no pupil had been before her for caning although it was common knowledge she had a cane wrapped in brown paper for use if needed. One day two girls were brought to school by the police for stealing and Miss Gray told the Constable to leave the girls with her and she would deal out any punishment. She placed a sheet of paper and pen in front of each girl and told them to record all that they had stolen. After filling in the page the girls were told in a stern voice "I mean all of it". The girls then started to write over the page feverishly. Miss Gray then asked Mrs Franklyn, the secretary to go to her cupboard and fetch out the cane. Mrs. Franklyn went to search the cupboard but all she could find was a very long pole used to open sash windows but wrapped in brown paper.

The horror on the girls' faces was a picture when she entered the room carrying the pole!

The door which separated the Boys' and Girls' school was nicknamed "Hebe's Man Trap".

The girls' Hall was used for Christmas Concerts with plays produced by most classes and on Parent Open Days when Needlework, Craft and Art were displayed. As the building started to deteriorate due to subsidence, the Hall was placed out of bounds and the girls used to share the boys' Hall for events. The classroom used for 2A was also unused due to the ceiling being unsafe. Test boring on the site near to this room indicated a depth of 80ft with no firm substance.

In the 1950s Miss Oak, Jean Hollingsworth and others undertook to arrange series of courses for school leavers each afternoon with a multitude of subjects covering, First Aid, Literature, Shakespeare Plays and Poetry, Elizabethan Times and Dancing, Rope Splicing, Fitting washer on Tap etc.

Miss Oak's recalls whilst she was on playground duty, a parent and well known character came through from the boys entrance and she promptly got hold of him by his jacket and hauled him out of the school. At some of the lessons the following answers were given by individuals

What is a Tourniquet used for -- to stop breeding!

Who used the first English Prayer Book -- The Prostitutes?

Memories of Jane Hyldon King

Pupil from 1962-64

When it comes to looking back at our childhood, most relish the fact that they were the happiest days of one's life, others just want to forget those days or have no interest in them.

For me, it was like opening up Pandora's Box, I couldn't wait to go to what was referred to as "Big School" and join my sister Christine and her friends. Although I was only at Armstrong for two years I hold some cherished memories of my time at the school and kept a small diary of my time there.

Going to school for me wasn't at all difficult. I can recall so many events from my first day starting school at Littlecoates in 1955 in the West Marsh. In 1962 I followed my brothers Byron and John and sisters June and Christine on to Armstrong Secondary School.

Leaving Littlecoates and going to Armstrong was so strange; being in a mixed school environment from the age of five then stepping into an all girls school was certainly something different. It didn't take long for me to realise that I preferred all girls to a mixed school environment. There was none of the rough and tumble and bullying tactics where the boys didn't think twice about pushing you over outside the school gates.

What a difference being in an all girl environment; we soon settled down to become young well balanced and well behaved young ladies.

Reading the media coverage in the archives at Grimsby Library about the new build of Armstrong School in 1929, I was amazed by the old fashioned attitude of those in power, aimed at young ladies, when deciding to build this school.

I Quote;

"At the new school in Armstrong Street, Grimsby girls are to be instructed in the art of housekeeping, they will be taught how to cook, how to launder in a thoroughly equipped laundry & kitchen. The husbands of the future will have a good deal to thank Armstrong Street for."

I often wonder what it would have been like in the early days coming to Armstrong school, for me regardless of the attitudes of the politicians of the day; I did enjoy cookery and visiting the school flat and spending time helping to clean it. The flat consisted of a large kitchen with pans hanging from the ceiling with a shelf with many different weighted irons on. There was a large sink, with draining board and large wooden table. Also there was a pantry stocked with pots and kitchen equipment of the day.

I remember a small bedroom with a picture of the Queen on one wall and a picture of Jesus on the other. There was a small single bed with the old fashioned green quilt or what was known as an eiderdown on the top and a small set of drawers on the other side of the bed. As students we would go into the flat and sweep and dust and make sure it was kept clean and tidy. I can remember one pupil being sent there to rest because she wasn't very well.

The kitchen was used for cookery lessons and we were taught how to take care of ourselves, the importance of keeping clean and tidy and basic hygiene.

Then we would learn the basics of how to handle food and gradually we would be allowed to cook and prepare things like stews, sausages and mashed potatoes, salads, bake scones, apple pies, jams & lemon tarts and my favourite at the time, coconut macaroons. Cookery was fun, although we had to bring all our ingredients in for whatever meal we were to prepare.

For me, my domestic skills had already been taught by my mother from an early age. Coming from a large family we learnt how to cook, clean and help with the laundry. My father taught me how to change a tyre on a bike and look after chickens and clean the chicken run as well as how to grow vegetables in our large garden.

On my first day at Armstrong in September 1962, we were taken into the school hall and introduced to our teacher. Then we were told what school house we had been put into and mine was "St Cecelia's" and the colour was "Blue" and what tended to happen was all your family would be placed in the same colour house, so I followed a tradition and went into the blue house.

On arriving into my class, the first thing I noticed were the large windows filling the class with so much daylight. Then seeing row upon row of two seater wooden desks, with a blackboard that almost filled one side of the class.

I liked the idea of having a basic school uniform, consisting of a white blouse and navy gymslip or skirt and a navy blue tie with a pale blue stripe, although not many pupils actually wore them.

My first year at Armstrong will always stand out in my mind and my first class teacher was Miss Parton who many will remember as the music teacher. She was a very tall slim lady with short black hair and wore spectacles and I can remember her always wearing red lipstick. She was always kind and her love of music resonated throughout the school.

Most of us can look back and often relate why we enjoyed certain lessons. For me music was a passion and she introduced many pupils to all styles of music from Peter and the Wolf to Gilbert & Sullivan. She also taught us a lot of traditional music, with songs as varied as Kathleen Ferrier's "Blow the Wind Southerly" and Scottish folk songs.

Many former students, I am sure will remember songs like Cargoes, The Earl King and Lynden Lee. These songs still remain some of my favourites even after all these years.

I still remember most of the teachers that taught me and many I am sure will remember Mrs Dixon who taught History at the school. Again a memorable teacher

who was passionate in the way she related to history and often kept us spell bound with her stories. I remember her coming into the class, she was stern and many pupils would be frightened of her, she was so strict, yet she was such a good teacher. She would move a pupil at the front of the class out of their seat, sit on the desk with her feet on the seat and she would take us back into history for the next hour.

Whether it was the "Roman Empire" or the "Tudors" I was always spell bound by her style of teaching and she still remains one of my favourite teachers and history remains one of my favourite pastimes.

When it came to Maths, I remember disliking this subject and couldn't believe it when I found out we were to be taught by a male teacher. Over the years Armstrong girls had, by tradition, female teachers, so this was a first for the school. His name was Mr Chadwick, although new to the Girls' School, he actually taught in the Armstrong Boys' School and had been moved to work within the girl's school. From a young girl's view he was quite a dishy looking guy he helped me to understand the basics of Maths as I found his teaching style helped me enormously and for the first time I started to enjoy Maths.

Armstrong School Houses

On my arrival at Armstrong we were all placed in one of four houses mine being St Cecilia's. It was fun being part of a house team and I soon became a house captain.

The houses would come together for annual sports days and would gain points for winning. We would have netball tournaments, swimming competitions, along with competitions around Christmas and Easter when we would have to make Christmas cards or hats that were judged for the best design. Over the year they would count up all the points gained from every pupil and the winning house would win the annual "House Cup" Sports.

For many years sports played a huge role within schools, with every school competing against each other. Every school wanted to pride itself at being the best whether at Netball, Football, Cricket or Athletics. Armstrong was no different and I can remember for many years Armstrong being well known for its sporting achievements.

When I started Armstrong, like my sisters I went on to play netball and like Christine at one stage played for the senior team. I also swam for the school at the old Eleanor Street Baths following on to the new Scartho baths and can remember winning a backstroke competition. I know that both of my brothers who attended Armstrong won many cups and medals for different sporting achievements and all three of us sisters won trophies and medals in netball, one being "The American Tournament Cup" along with junior and senior netball league cups within our own year groups. I believe this helped to shape our lives at the same time as keeping us fit and healthy, which is sadly lacking in most schools today.

When I first arrived at Armstrong there had been many years of rumours that one day a new school would be built and I can remember my sister always telling me that by the time I had reached secondary school, it would possibly be a new school.

But after many delays in starting the new build I did eventually get the opportunity to go to Armstrong for two years before going to Hereford. I was so pleased that I had had the experience of attending such a remarkable good caring girl's school that did have a huge impact on my life.

It is so easy to say that going to a new school gave me far more advantages in education and yes, Hereford was a remarkable school with new technology and a building that had everything you could ever dream of. We had new sport facilities, two sports halls, one in-door facility and one that was open on one side to the elements.

We also had huge sports fields for outside activities of football and athletics, two sets

of kitchens for cookery, with working spaces for each individual with your own cooker and equipment.

Two Science labs with all state of the art equipment and what really impressed me were the Business study rooms with each desk opening up with its own typewriter.

It was a little like an Aladdin's cave, so coming from Armstrong school, you couldn't help but be in awe of the facilities.

Yes we had a new school with out of this world equipment and better life skills and opportunities, but being part of a small Girls' school I believed it did shape the way forward for young women.

Snippets from my diary

28th February 1964

Had needlework today – While using the hand sewing machine and not looking what I was doing I trapped my thumb and the needle went partly through the nail, breaking the needle in two. I was very upset and my teacher Mrs Mellows made sure I was ok.

17th March 1964

Our class was selected to perform a play called "The Spophems". We had a couple of weeks to learn our parts then we performed it at the South Parade Methodist Chapel in Yarborough Street, just across the road from the Grimsby Hospital.

- Mrs Spophem – Jane Hyldon
- Mr Spophem – Margaret Brown
- The Burglar – Jean Charlesworth
- The Dog – Pam Bagshaw
- The Cat – Linda Harmer
- The Policeman – Margaret Hart

March 1964

I received my Bronze Medal Award for swimming in the hall. I had to swim 24 widths of the Scartho baths, jump off the second board with night clothes on and tread water for 5 minutes. I received a medal and certificate.

Jane Hyldon and her sister, June Hyldon – both were house Captains of St Cecilia's

March 1964

Became school captain for St Cecilia's house and presented with my badge.

No Date

Armstrong girls' choir performed at the Town Hall signing songs from Orpheus & the Underworld and my favourite song was "What is life to me without thee?"

The choir also performed at the Central Hall jointly with other schools.

The choir was made up of young ladies from each year and both my sister Christine & I were part of the choir and we would practise at home with our other close friends who were also part of the choir.

No Date

During my time at Armstrong we all went through the stages of following the style of music from singers like Del Shannon to The Beatles. Also in my diary I make reference to a prank several of us played on our friends at school.

My sister Christine, Diane Robinson, Janet Powell, Shelia Tyson and a couple more, told all our school friends that we had gone down to London Airport to see the Beatles coming back from a tour abroad. They all believed us until eventually we did tell the truth, but had fun pretending we had met the Beatles. What it was like to be young!

So for me my memories are still quite strong and the day the school closed, there was not a dry eye to be seen. We never lost touch with our school friends although many went to different schools than Hereford.

During the 70s I remember attending the first Armstrong School reunion with my sister Christine, our school friend Janet Powell and my mother-in- law Kathleen King.

Many former Armstrong girls met up on the school site and we spent a wonderful afternoon chatting about the old days. Over the years we did go on to have further reunions but it was not just for Armstrong school but all who lived and worked in the West Marsh.

During 2011, I was contacted by one of my sister Christine's school friends Lesley McCormick who was in her class and knowing that my sister had died some years ago, she approached me, and invited me along to their regular Armstrong get together. I was impressed to see so many friends had taken time to keep in touch over the years, and pleased that they had taken time out to invite me. Although not in their class and two years younger, it was like going back in time and sharing stories and photographs of our time at Armstrong School, we still meet bi-monthly for lunch.

Mrs Joyce Beedham (Nee Dean)

Extracts from her exercise book 1942 (age 14)

A Civilian In Wartime
4 Sept 1942

A civilian in Wartime is a very important person as there are many rules and regulations.

There are Ration Books, Clothing Coupons and various other books, if you lose your coupons there is a fine of one shilling, if you cannot afford it you are imprisoned for a month or more, also carry your Identity-Card or you are fined as well.

Then there are some other things such as Air-Raids, if people are bombed out and they are unhurt they claim compensation and receive clothes when they go to the Rest Centre until relations take them in, If they are in difficulty, they go to the Citizens Advice Bureau.

There is a civilian tin hat which everyone has not got yet, they are supplied by the peoples work, the gas masks are given to everyone, if they are damaged they have to pay for them. Everyone also have earplugs. All people worry about the blackout if not a fine of two pounds is imposed. If an Incendiary bomb falls you could be burnt, if you are burnt then you go to the Wardens Post where they would attend to it, you would put it out with a Stirrup Pump or some sand. Also leave all your clothing handy in case of an Air- Raid.

Rules Of My School
22 Oct 1942

The Rules throughout the day beginning from nine fifteen are; Do not talk while in the Cloak Room and do not wash your hands when you go into prayers you have to be level with the window or the pillar, you have not to make a noise when you come out of the Hall. The lessons begin, first, it is Arithmetic you get all your articles out including a library book, if you talk or murmur you have to stay in at four-o clock. Then break, drink milk over the basket, take milk tops off the bottles and throw them away, also save your straws as they will do for the afternoon. Then, at home time you tidy up the classroom so the Caretaker has less to do. There are two more rules that have not been mentioned, one is not to play under the windows or you disturb the people who are working. The other is not to bring cases to school. We have rules because if there were no rules the school would be upside down and that means the girls would do as they liked.

How I Can Save Fuel In My Home
17 Nov 1942

Are you looking towards your fuel target? Then here are my hints

Share the oven with a neighbour and both pay expenses. Do not have so many baths one day is sufficient instead of two. Go to bed earlier than normal and do not have a fire or light burning. Do all your cooking on a Tuesday, Thursday, Saturday and Sunday then you can cook for the next day instead of wasting coal & gas for the following day.

When you are cleaning the hearth, sift your cinders, if no cinder sifter is available take an old box with the bottom out and fasten some wire netting over the bottom this will make a good sifter and you can use the cinders again. Do not have fresh water every time anyone gets washed, let them wash in the same water unless they are ill, and you can burn wood and potato peelings it makes a big warm fire. Do not keep washing clothes unless you have to as it is not necessary.

Do not let anyone leave the light on, and try to go to bed without a light on, this is very economical. So please be easy on Fuel it is precious these days.

Memories of other pupils

Mrs Betty Houlton (Nee Riggall)
1933-37

I was born in Charlton St on 23 June 1923 and recall going to Armstrong St School infants and then seniors; I left school in October 1937.

The start time was 9.00am and finished at 4.00pm except on Fridays when we had a short break and finished at 1.30pm. We walked to school from our house. The class sizes were approx 35 girls.

We were taught to play tennis on the Boulevard.

We regularly took part in the Cleethorpes Music Festival with pronunciation and poetry.

I recall a dentist used to be up the stairs.

I recall the Interschool Sports Day was held on Old Clee fields and I hold a medal for winning the Netball Championship in 1936/37 as Captain.

Most teachers arrived at school on their bikes and the girls would take their bikes and place them in the bike rack.

Miss Gray was strict but fair.

Mrs Sheila Copley (Nee Hubbard)
1946-51

I was born in 1935 at Clarke Ave. I went to Armstrong St School from 1946-51 and walked from home each day and returned home for dinner.

I recall the bad winter in 1947 when we walked to school in waist deep snow only to be returned home with the school closed because of no coke for the heating boilers.

The size of the classes was approx. 35-40 pupils. There was no homework given out.

I was made a prefect at school and was appointed head girl. On the schools 21st anniversary I was allowed to cut the birthday cake with Headmistress Miss Gray and other prefects of the school in attendance.

I recall the following teachers:

Miss Disney used to walk around with a ruler which she used on offenders by hitting them on the knuckles or the back of their legs.

Miss Shatford used to run the School choir.

Miss Harvey was the netball teacher and used to walk about by prancing on her tip toes

Miss Hammond was short and stubby

Girls hanging a farewell banner on the last ever day of school

ARMSTRONG STREET GIRLS' SCHOOL.

Name................... Date of Birth... 9.6.37... Admitted from................... Age on Admittance... 11.12.9...

	Class... IIIA... Date... Feb. 1951 Form Mistress...		Class... 3A... Date... July 1951 Form Mistress...		Class... 4A... Date... March 1952 Form Mistress...		Class... 4A... Date... July 1952 Form Mistress...	
	Report on First Half Year ending... Feb. 1951	Exams. Act-ual. / Max.	Report on Second Half Year ending... July 1951	Exams. Act-ual. / Max.	Report on First Half Year ending... March 1952	Exams. Act-ual. / Max.	Report on Second Half Year ending... July 1952	Exams. Act-ual. / Max.
English ...		69½ 90		73 90		73 90		76 90
FRENCH ...		13½ 20		13½ 20		13½ 20		12 20
Literature ...		14½ 20		17 20		14½ 20		14 20
Verse Speaking ...		10 10		10 10		10 10		10 10
Reading ...		18 20		18 20		17 20		19 20
Arithmetic ...		44½ 100		54 100		33 100		C30 100
Geography ...		15 20		14½ 20		11 20		18½ 20
History ...		18½ 20		16½ 20		16 20		18½ 20
Biology ...		18 20		17½ 20		10 20		17½ 20
Needlework ...		17 20		18 20		17 20		17 20
Handwork ...		14½ 20		13 20		12 20		13 20
ART ...		12½ 20		20 20		17½ 20		17½ 20
Domestic Science ... MUSIC		14½ 20		20 20		20 20		16 20
Drill and Games ...		16½ 20		15½ 20		15½ 20		16 20
Total ...		28¾ 400		288½ 400		265 400		278 400
Position in Class ...	11 out of 49		12 out of 49		25 out of 43		14 out of 24	
Attendances ...	150 out of 150		356 out of 364		257 out of 258		343 out of 344	
Punctuality ...	Times Late		Times Late		Times Late		Times Late	

Report on Work and Conduct ...

Class Teacher ...

Headmistress ...

Parent's Signature ...

Example Of An Early School Report 1949

Report on half-year ending .... July 1940.

Form ... IV^A   No. in Form ... 31   Form Mistress ... G Brookes

	Remarks	Position in Form	EXAMS. Act.	EXAMS. Poss.
English	Excellent work throughout school life	10	76	120
Literature	Excellent	1	28	30
Verse Speaking ...	Excellent		10	10
Reading	Very good - clear voice		9	10
Arithmetic	Good - works well.	9	57	100
Geography	Quite good -	14	20	40
History	Good work.	16	27	40
Biology	Very good - steady worker	3	32	40
French Art	Fairly good - works well	10	17	30
Needlework	Has worked very well		33	40
Music	Quite good.	13	16½	30
Domestic Science ...	Become first & always works well. Excellent Barbara deserves	1	36.	40
P. E. and Games ...	Very Good works hard	16	20	
Religious Knowledge	Very good.	7	28½	30
General Knowledge	Good.		15½	20

Later example of a Girls School Report

Total Marks Gained 421½

Total Marks Possible 600

Percentage 70.2%

Position in Form .... 5th.

Attendance { Actual .... Possible ....

Punctuality ... Excellent .... Times Late ....

Form Mistress's Report on Work and Conduct ....
Barbara has worked exceptionally well this term with pleasing results. Of good appearance she has a pleasant manner and is at all times willing and helpful.   G Brookes

Head Mistress's Remarks ....

Parent's Signature ... A. Routhley

Register of Teaching Staff

NAME	SUBJECT TAUGHT	START	FINISH
Miss E M Alvey		Sept 1942	Feb 1944
Miss Marjorie Ayres	P T Teacher Netball	Aug 1932	Sept 1939
Miss Dorothy Barningham	English	July 1952	Sept 1955
Miss Jennie D Baker	Music	June 1934	Aug 1938
J D Maureen Baxter		Aug 1938	
Miss Ena A Bee		July 1952	Aug 1955
Audrey Benton		Sept 1938	Feb 1942
Audrey Benson		Sept 1945	Aug 1948
Miss M Berry		Sept 1941	Nov 1943
Jean Blakely		July 1954	Sept 1956
Connie Bonnello	Headmistress 1952-1958	June 1952	Apr 1958
Miss Margaret Bottomley	Domestic-	Aug 1936	Aug 1938
Miss Mary C Brakenridge	Cookery	Jan 1930	Dec 1930
Mrs Gladys Brookes (nee Bright)	Maths	Oct 1929	Aug 1936
Miss G Brooks		June 1948	
Miss Joan B Brown		July 1952	Aug 1954
Miss Mary Brydges		July 1948	Aug 1952
Miss Edna M L Buchanan		Jan 1949	Dec 1949
Mrs M F Burton		June 1942	Sept 1942
Mrs B Cammack (nee Dixon)			Nov 1959
Miss Mary Carter-White	P T Teacher	June 1935	Sept 1940
Mrs B Chablo		Apr 1959	Dec 1960
Miss I Chapman		Oct 1929	Jan 1934
Miss P Chester	Domestic – Housewifery	May 1932	
Mrs H Chester-Watts	Domestic	Jan 1942	Sept 1945
Miss Zara B C Chrispin		Oct 1946	Apr 1947
Miss Ivy S Clark		Sept 1936	May 1942
Mrs J Vicky Coates (nee Mowat)	Domestic	Mar 1941	Oct 1949
Miss J Cotterill	p/t Piano	May 1954	
Miss Marie Crothers	Cookery	Apr 1939	Dec 1941
Miss Phyllis M D Disney	Headmistress 1958-1964	Aug 1930	July 1964
Miss Rene Dales		Sept 1936	Mar 1940
Mrs F Davies			Aug 1964
Miss A K Dennis		Sept 1951	Aug 1952
Mrs Jessie Dixon	History	Nov 1945	1951
Miss M K Dowse		Oct 1931	
Miss T E Drury		July 1952	
Freda Dulson	Drama, English		
Mrs Audrey E Dyson (nee Andrews)		Sept 1945	Sept 1946
Miss Joan M Ellis		July 1948	Apl 1951
Mrs E Joyce Hollingsworth (nee Ellis)		Aug 1940	
Mrs. C M Farrow (nee Watson)	French	Aug 1940	Dec 1953
Miss Mary W Fidell			Aug 1952
Miss F A Findley		Sept 1938	Sept 1941
Margaret Franklyn (nee Foster)	Secretary	Nov 1949	
Miss L R Furneval		May 1957	Apr 1958
Hebe Gray	Headmistress 1929-1952	Sept 1929	Dec 1951
Miss A Gorbutt		Sept 1961	Aug 1963
Mrs Gormley		Apr 1940	
Miss I Gott		Oct 1929	Oct 1932
Miss J M Goy		Apr 1958	Aug 1960
Miss E J Hammond		Oct 1943	
Miss M Hammond		Sept 1958	Dec 1958
Linda D Haswell		Sept 1938	

NAME	SUBJECT TAUGHT	START	FINISH
Miss Barbara S Harrison		Sept 1938	Aug 1943
Miss Enid B Harvey		Aug 1940	
Miss Linda D Haswell		Aug 1937	
Miss Winifred K Hemsley		Aug 1930	Aug 1931
Miss B Hewson		Nov 1946	
Miss E Hickton		Sept 1956	Apr 1957
Miss V J Holloway		Sept 1963	June 1964
Mrs E J Hollingsworth (nee Ellis)		July 1948	Aug 1952
Miss Cissie J Howells	Domestic	Jan 1932	
Wendy Hunt		July 1954	
Mrs A M Hunter		Apr 1961	
Mrs Jenny Hutton	Choir & Music	Sept 1938	Jan 1941
Doreen Jackson (nee Mumby)	P T Netball coach		
Mrs E M Jackson		Apr 1962	
Miss Rhonna L Jeffreys	Domestic	Sept 1936	Feb 1939
Miss Julia G Johnson		Aug 1945	Dec 1946
Mrs Ruth F Jones (nee Parrott)	English	July 1948	June 1953
Miss Kemp			
Miss P A Kennington		Jan 1958	Aug 1958
Miss Margaret S Kerruish	Cookery + Housewifery	Aug 1934	Sept 1936
Miss E M Kilburn			Aug 1945
P Lager		Jan 1931	Sept 1931
T M Lonerhan		Aug 1944	
Phyliss G Lane	Deputy Head 1929-1952	Oct 1929	Aug 1954
Miss J Mason			Dec 1960
Shirley McDonald			
Miss M McCandlish		Sept 1949	Dec 1949
Mrs Mellows (nee Potts)	Biology		June 1959
Hettie Metcalf		Sept 1938	
D Molyneux		Oct 1932	
Mrs Catherine Montgomery		Sept 1950	Aug 1952
Mrs G J Morrison		Sept 1957	Dec 1957
Miss D Mulhall		Sept 1960	
Miss D E Mumby			Aug 1960
Miss Joan M V Nobbs		July 1952	Aug 1958
Mrs A Noseworthy		Sept 1956	Apr 1957
Mrs B Noxon		Oct 1946	Jan 1947
Miss Betty O Brien	Cooking	July 1952	
Mrs S Palmer		Jan 1953	Aug 1955
Miss J M Parkinson		Sept 1952	Oct 1952
Mrs S Parrot			June 1957
Miss B M Parton	Music	Sept 1960	
Mrs June Partridge (nee Hammond)			Apr 1955
Mrs A Pestrjetzily		Oct 1954	
Miss C M Picard			Sept 1963
Miss Miriam Pickwell	History	Oct 1929	Nov 1947
Mrs S Pinchbeck (nee Goodwin)		June 1954	May 1962
Miss C Potterton		Sept 1960	Aug 1961
Miss Rene L Potterton		Aug 1933	Feb 1935
Miss G M Potts		Sept 1959	
Miss Pat L M Presswood	Needlework, Maths	July 1948	Apr 1950
Miss Dorothy M Reynolds		Oct 1942	Aug 1950
Miss E M Rhodes		July 1932	Sept 1937
Mrs Jean Robins (nee Oak)	Biology, Geog, Needlework	Sept 1947	1959
Miss K P Ryder		Oct 1929	Aug 1932

NAME	SUBJECT TAUGHT	START	FINISH
Miss V B Sanderson			Aug 1940
Miss F R Saunders		June 1945	Sept 1945
Miss Florence E Schofield		Apr 1930	
Mrs E E Scully	Cooking	Jan 1953	Jan 1964
Miss J Sealey	Domestic subjects	Sept 1939	
Miss Grace E M Shatford	Music	Sept 1941	
Miss Janet C Shaw	Needlework	Aug 1940	Aug 1956
Miss E M Siddy		Sept 1959	
Brenda Skinns			
Mrs M Smalley	p/t Piano	Sept 1956	Feb 1960
Miss J C Smith	Domestic subjects	Aug 1938	
Mrs W Smith	Needlework	Jun 1959	Apr 1961
Miss D Smithies		July 1958	July 1959
Miss Sadie Spendiff	Sewing	Jan 1934	Aug 1948
Miss Kathleen A Taylor		July 1952	Apr 1954
Miss Margaret Thompson	Domestic - Housewifery	Oct 1929	Dec 1929
Audrey Thorp		1960	
Miss J Trueman		Sept 1958	Sept 1961
Mrs Morag I Towriss		Sept 1948	
Miss Jessie Turner		Jan 1930	Aug 1964
Miss B R Uhrmacher		Sept 1960	
Miss M Verity			Aug 1959
Nancy Waite			
Miss M Walker			Apr 1954
Mrs Walkley		May 1940	
Miss Lona Wilkinson	English	Sept 1947	
Miss E M Windsor	Domestic Subjects	Aug 1938	Apr 1941
Miss Y Whitby	P/t Pianist	Jan 1950	
Miss W G Woods		Jan 1958	Aug 1960
Mrs G Woodword (nee Allen)		Aug 1943	May 1945
Miss Edna M Woolley		Aug 1937	
Miss L Wrightson		Nov 1943	

Male Teachers

NAME	SUBJECT TAUGHT	START	FINISH
Mr Roy Beverage	Geography	July 1950	Sept 1952
Mr J T Chadwick	Mathematics	Sept 1962	Aug 1964
Mr Robert O Jones	Geography	Sept 1950	Sept 1952
Mr F J Partridge	Geography	July 1950	Sept 1952
Mr Maurice Peers	Geography	Dec 1950	Sept 1952
Mr Charles Strickland	Art	July 1950	Sept 1952

13: The Demise Of The School

This Chapter hoped to remove any speculation on the cause of structural failure leading to the eventual demolition of the school. Yet, despite detailed scrutiny of records, no specific details are listed, and the investigation has been hindered by the absence of many important documents.

This chapter attempts to explain the construction of the building foundations from the initial trial bores of the strata to the design structure of the foundations of the school. The structural problems due to settlement happened as early as 1932 when reports of defects of cracks in the walls were discussed at frequent intervals by the Education Committee meetings with subsequent proposals for work to be carried out to address the problem but to no avail.

The details of these meetings have been included in this chapter but none show any evidence of any significant detail as to the cause of the subsidence. In 1956, at the instigation of the Ministry of Education, the committee sought the services of a well renowned consultant, Mr Maurice Nachshen, who submitted his detailed report to the Education Committee on 4th March 1957.

Unfortunately the contents of this highly important, yet sensitive, document remains a mystery. Despite an extensive search in the council archives, Borough Engineers and Education Committee documents, no trace of its existence has been found, neither has it been printed in any reports or details from the findings published. Why would a documents so important be destroyed?

Construction of the School Foundations

Five trial bores were bored on the proposed site by Messrs F Smith & Sons (Well Borers) in April 1926, the results of which are shown overleaf.

The average working water level was 15-26ft in each trial bore position.

The construction drawings show a total of 164 piles intermittently spaced around the building. The concrete piles consisted of columns of five ½" dia mild steel rods with tie rings of ¼" dia spaced 5ft apart placed in 10" dia. bore holes with an 8" dia steel tube x 20ft long remaining in the bottom section of the bore hole as the concrete is then poured in, with 12" of rods above the surface to form a raft foundation.

The first signs of structural problems were soon visible as cracks started to appear in walls shortly after the plastered walls had been painted inside. The problems that were eventually to lead to the demolition of the school were to become apparent. Later on cracks started to appear in walls, where the entrance to the boy's school, the stone lintel bearing the legend "BOYS" had a massive crack through it. Having to necessitate timber beams shoring up the entrance, the undulating surface of the corridor, which ran around the quadrangle, all sounded the death knell for the school's future.

At the Education Committee held on 21st September 1932 it was reported that there were defects in the walls at Armstrong St School, but this was postponed to a future meeting.

At the Education Sub Committee held on 10th July 1934 the Chairman reported with reference to the buildings of Armstrong St School on the action he had taken. It was resolved that the action of the Chairman be confirmed and that the school Building Committee be recommended to have a survey of the whole building made by the Borough Engineer.

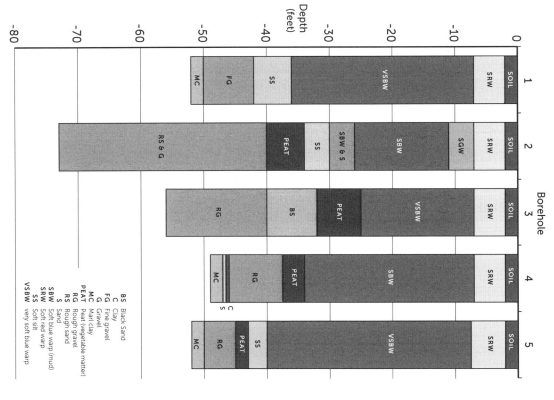

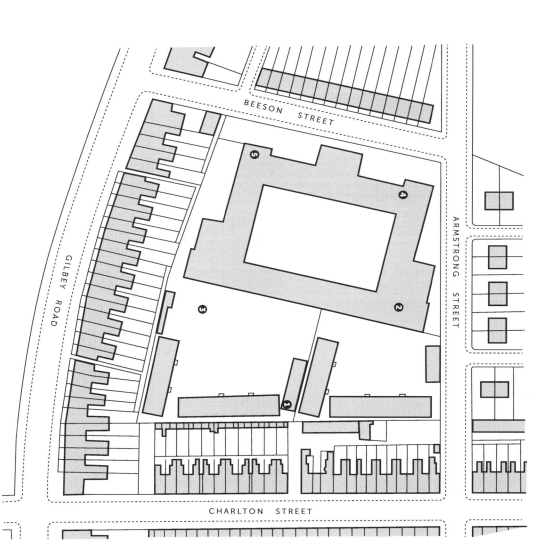

Results of Trial Bores in 1926 on proposed site

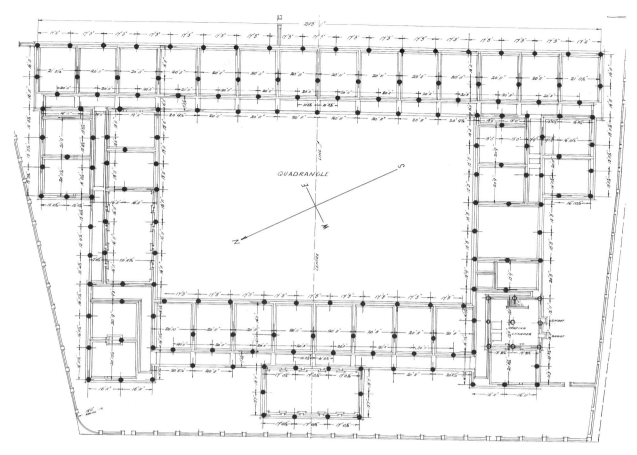

Foundation plan showing setting out of concrete piles

At an Education Sub Committee on 6th Feb 1935 a report from the Borough Engineer and Surveyor was presented with regards to the subsidence at Armstrong St School.

At a meeting of the School Management Committee on 3rd February 1937, the Chairman, Councillor I Abraham, drew the attention of the sub committee to a report on further evidence of subsidence at Armstrong St School. It was resolved that the report be referred to the Borough Engineer & Surveyor for his observations.

In May 1941, the Borough Surveyor had steel points fixed at various cracks in order that any further movement could be measured by caliper measurement.

At an Education Finance and General Sub Committee on 19th October 1954 a report submitted by the Borough Engineer relating to the continued subsidence at Armstrong Secondary Modern School stating that a number of bore holes and a careful examination of the foundations would have to be made, the cost of which is likely to have exceeded £500.

It was resolved that the Borough Engineer be authorised to carry out a thorough inspection of the building, including the examination of the foundations at various points and the making of boreholes.

At a meeting of the Education Committee on 12 December 1955 the Borough Engineer reported on the proposed alterations of Armstrong Secondary Modern Schools and the possibility of obtaining a further site. It was resolved that the Borough Engineer be authorised to make trial bore holes forthwith on the 17 ½ acres of committees land in Macaulay Street at an estimated cost of £300 and to report to this committee as soon as possible.

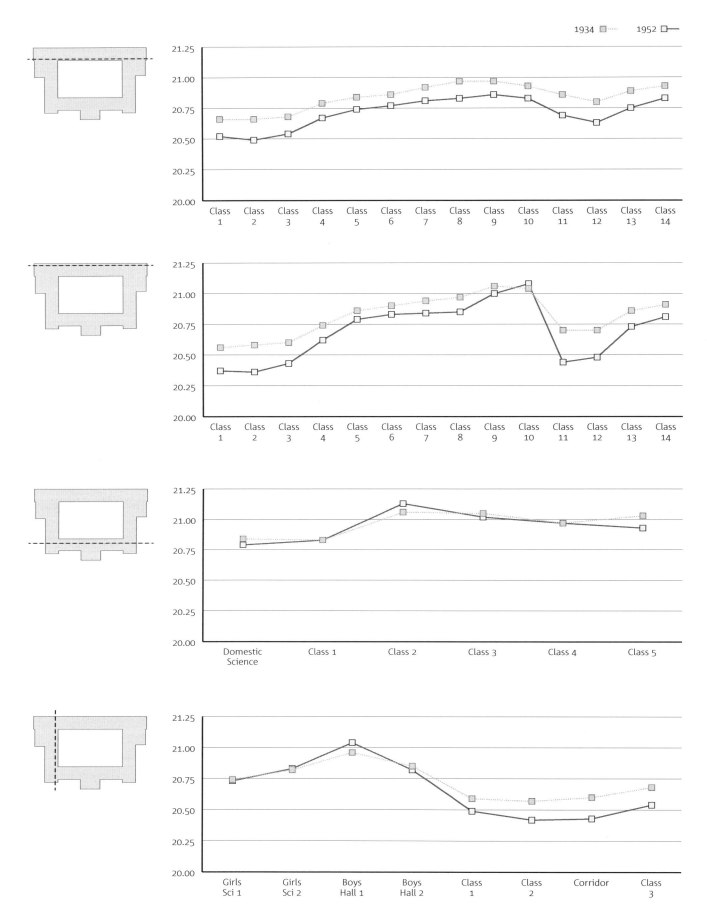

A plan drawing of the school deposited at the Borough Engineers showed readings taken in 1934 and 1952 at set locations in the school which enabled this subsidence comparison to be made.

(ii) That the Director be asked to approach the Ministry of Education with a view to obtaining approval in principle to the proposed building of a new 4-form entry mixed school on the above site pending the results of the bore hole tests with consideration to the question of drainage.

A meeting of the Education Committee sat on the 20th February 1956 to discuss an alternative site for Armstrong St School. It was reported that a letter had been received from the Ministry of Education stating that the 17,364 acres of land appear prima facie suitable as a site to replace the two existing schools.

At a meeting of the Education Committee a detailed report submitted by the Borough Engineer regarding a proposed site in Macaulay Lane it was resolved that this matter be differed and that the Borough Engineer be requested to attend the next meeting of the Sub Committee.

At a meeting of the Education Committee on 19th March 1956 the Borough Engineer reported on the existing Armstrong Secondary Modern School and the proposed site for a new school. He stated that if the existing school were remodelled at an estimated cost of some £100,000 settlement would probably continue necessitating continuous expenditure on repair work. If a new school were built on the proposed new site in Macaulay Lane additional costs amounting to approximately £20,000 would be incurred on piling, special foundation work, drainage and road works making a total of approximately £210,000.

It was resolved that following the report of the Borough Engineer, the Committees approval in principle of the erection of a new 4 form entry mixed school on the site in Macaulay Lane be confirmed.

(ii) That the Ministry of Education be asked to approve in principle the additional costs in respect of piling, special foundation work, drainage and roadworks amounting to approximately £20,000.

At a meeting of the Education committee on 16th April 1956 the Borough Engineer submitted a periodical inspection report stating that, although certain points required the attention of the clerk of works, the movement during the past six- seven months has been very small and no new signs of settlement were noted.

At a meeting of the Sub Committee on 23rd October 1956 it was reported that a letter had been received from the Ministry of Education:

"I am directed by the Ministry of Education to refer to the visit recently made by Mr Halstead to inspect the buildings of the Armstrong Secondary Modern Schools. After consideration of Mr Halsted's report, the Minister considers that the Authority should at an early date, seek the opinion of a consultant Architect fully acquainted with soil mechanics and modern foundation techniques as well as practical structural considerations before further measures to remedy the situation are contemplated.

The Minister suggests that his Officers should discuss the choice of a suitable consultant with Officers of the Authority in the near future".

With the approval of the Chairman of the Education Committee the Borough Engineer and the Director of Education visited the Ministry of Education on 10th October 1956.

Resolved: That, as suggested by the Ministry of Education, the services of a Consultant Engineer be engaged and that the Director of Education be authorised on behalf of the Education Committee to engage Mr Maurice Nachshen BSc, MICE and to proceed with the arrangement forthwith.

At a meeting of the Education Committee held on 4th March 1957 a consultants' report on subsidence of Armstrong Secondary Modern School was submitted from Maurice Nachshen, Bsc MICE MISE, on the damage by subsidence to Armstrong St School and means of arresting it.

© Grimsby Telegraph

*the school must go
... it is the fault of
our predecessors*

It was resolved that the closure of Armstrong St Secondary Modern School and the erection of a 4 form entry secondary mixed school on the site to the north of Macaulay Street extension be approved in principle.

The authority be given for the payment of £411-10s-4d to Maurice Nachshen on account of his work from October 1956 to February 1957 in connection with his inspection report on Armstrong Secondary Modern School.

On 2nd April 1957 The Chairman of the Governors, Councillor G H Pearson announced to the public at the Armstrong Secondary Modern Girls' School Speech Day at the Town Hall that a new school, costing £200,000, is to be built in Macaulay Street replacing Armstrong St School.

"We have had a very big responsibility in deciding the school must go," he went on, "and you may ask why a school, which was only built in 1928, has had it; we have had this legacy with us for many years. It is the fault of our predecessors."

Councillor Pearson explained that the new school in Macaulay Street is to be built in three, four or five years and will be provided with plenty of recreational facilities and playing fields.

At an Education Committee held on 12th June 1964 Tenders were invited for the demolition of the main buildings of Armstrong St School following the transfer of all pupils to Hereford School in September 1964.

At the Education Committee held on 4th August 1964 it was decided that the tender from Mr M Phillips of Newark for the corporation to pay £437-10-0 for the demolition of Armstrong St Schools be accepted subject to the approval of the Borough Engineer.

Work commenced on demolishing the school during October 1964. Former pupils were spellbound as ink-stained desks, scarred with the initials of many of them, were piled in untidy heaps and classrooms stood open to the weather, their windows – focus of many a restless child's eyes – disappeared.

So ended the life of a school.

© Grimsby Telegraph